T

MW01196601

Trading Pain For Peace

Uprooting Pain Through Emotional Healing Prayer

Jim Gardner

2008

Special acknowledgment is gratefully given to Dr. Edward Smith for laying the conceptual foundation for this book. This book does not represent his ministry approach but does include many of the seminal ideas presented in his writings.

Trading Pain For Peace

Table of Contents

Preface   ix

Chapter 1   Emotions: Friends or Foes?   1

SECTION A: FACT-BASED EMOTIONS

Chapter 2   Overcoming Grief and Loss   15

Chapter 3   Eliminating Anger and Resentment   31

Chapter 4   Releasing Feelings of Sadness and
             Disappointment   45

Chapter 5   Dealing with Truth-based Guilt   59

SECTION B: BELIEF-BASED EMOTIONS

Chapter 6   Principles for Dealing with Belief-based
             Emotions   71

Chapter 7   Feelings of Fear and Anxiety   81

Chapter 8   Feelings of Loneliness and
             Abandonment   99

Chapter 9   Feelings of Hopelessness   111

Chapter 10   Feelings of Helplessness   121

Chapter 11   Feelings of Shame and Defilement   129

Chapter 12   Feelings of Hurt and Rejection   137

SECTION C: BIBLICAL PRINCIPLES

Chapter 13   Hindrances to Emotional
Healing Prayer   149

Chapter 14   Christian Discipleship and Counseling   157

Basic Principles of Prayer-Based Cognitive Therapy   168

Basic Principles of Emotional Healing Prayer   170

Belief-Based Feelings Chart   172

Fact-Based Feelings Chart   173

PREFACE

"For unto us a child is born, unto us a son is given; and the government shall be upon His shoulder: and His name shall be called Wonderful, Counselor, The mighty God, The everlasting Father, The Prince of Peace." Isaiah 9:6 (KJV)

This Scripture, made famous by Handel's *Messiah*, speaks of the coming Messiah, the Lord Jesus Christ, and describes Him as our "Wonderful Counselor." There have been many times in my life that I needed someone to comfort me or to give me advice or perspective in my life circumstances so that I could regain a sense of peace in my life. I worked as a professional counselor for over twenty-five years before I concluded that I could not help many people and I learned that the Lord Jesus is indeed the Wonderful Counselor who can heal people and set them free from emotional bondage. I have found that He is truly able to bring peace into my life as I learn to "cast all my cares upon" Him.

I received Jesus as my Savior as a child, and I grew up in a solid, Bible-teaching church where I learned to study the Bible and trust it as the foundation for my life. My parents were both Christians and provided me a loving home and a solid spiritual and moral base for life. However, I quickly began to realize that many Christians in our church had emotional struggles and were living defeated lives. The church leaders were godly men, who studied the Bible seriously but had no idea how to help the struggling believers in their church to overcome sinful behaviors and emotional struggles. This set me on a journey to try to understand human behavior through a search of the

Scriptures, through reading Christian counseling books, and through studying and pursuing a career in counseling. I studied psychology and counseling to learn how to help myself and other sincere believers in Jesus, to learn how we can live victorious lives. After receiving four degrees and spending twenty-five years as a mental health professional, however, I still found that it was difficult to help many Christians to experience victory in their lives. As important as I knew it was for people to be saved, it did not always release people from the bondage they had to their emotions and behaviors.

And then, after twenty-five years of discouragement, I learned some simple biblical principles that revolutionized my life and my professional practice. It has been very exciting for me to see patient after patient find freedom and peace rapidly, without me having to share my insights into their life circumstances. I have come to know the Lord Jesus experientially as "wonderful" and I am excited about sharing this knowledge with others. My motive for writing this book is to help you, the reader, to experience Jesus in the same way. He can do for you what I cannot do, what no counselor, psychologist, or doctor of any type can do for you or for me. He can break the chains of your past and release you from the negative emotions you carry. After all, this was the expressed mission of the Messiah according to the prophet Isaiah.

> The Spirit of the Lord God is upon me, Because the Lord has anointed me To bring good news to the afflicted; He has sent me to bind up the brokenhearted, To proclaim liberty to captives, And freedom to prisoners; To proclaim the favorable year of the Lord, And the day of vengeance of our God; To comfort all who mourn, To grant those who mourn in Zion, Giving them a garland instead of ashes, The oil of gladness instead of mourning, The mantle of praise instead of a spirit of fainting. Isaiah 61:1-3

As our Wonderful Counselor, the Lord wants to replace our pain with His peace. This is why the same prophet described the

Messiah as "the Prince of Peace" in Isaiah 9:6, and the angels in heaven appeared at His birth and proclaimed "peace on earth" (KJV, Luke 2:14). During His darkest hour on earth, when He was about to be crucified and forsaken by His Heavenly Father, He spoke words of comfort and peace to His disciples. In John 14:27 He said, "Peace I leave with you; My peace I give to you; not as the world gives, do I give to you. Let not your heart be troubled, nor let it be fearful." At the end of His final words spoken to the disciples that evening He concluded, "These things I have spoken to you, that in Me you may have peace" (John 16:33).

The apostle Paul repeatedly began his letters with the benediction "Grace to you and peace" (See Romans 1:7, 1 Corinthians 1:3, 2 Corinthians 1:2, Galatians 1:3, and Ephesians 1:2) and referred to the Lord Jesus as the "God of peace" and the "Lord of peace" (See Romans 15:33, Philippians 4:9, 2 Thessalonians 3:16) in his closing remarks in those letters. In clear and powerful terms he described "peace" as one of the fruits, or evidences, of the Holy Spirit in our lives (Galatians 5:22), and in 2 Thessalonians 3:16 Paul closed his letter by saying, "Now may the Lord of peace Himself continually grant you peace in every circumstance."

There can be no doubt that the Lord desires us to experience His peace; not just in a theoretical way but in a genuine way. Even in the midst of trials and difficult circumstances He desires us to experience a deep, genuine peace and calm as we learn to rest in Him and allow His Holy Spirit to comfort us. What a wonderful promise this is! My hope and prayer for each person who reads this book is that you will learn to replace your pain with "the peace of God that surpasses all comprehension", so that God will be glorified in your life and you will be able to produce the fruit in your life that He desires.

This book was written for those who know Jesus as their Savior but want to experience the "peace which surpasses all comprehension" (Philippians 4:7). It is my belief that these principles were given by the Lord to all believers, not just to a few select pastors and Christian counselors who are trying to shepherd the flock of God. All true believers have the Word of God, the Comforter, prayer, and the promise that the Holy Spirit "will guide you into all the truth" (John 16:13) and the Lord desires each of us to experience His peace and walk in His truth. I have found that these principles are good for helping others find peace and victory, and I have been able to find a great deal of peace in my own life as well.

I found it very helpful to pray with others while I was learning to use these principles, and sometimes I have learned that it helps to pray with a mature prayer partner when I am stuck and cannot seem to find the help I need. You will probably experience the same and should be able to find much peace as you learn to simply pray through some of your issues on your own. There will probably be times, however, when you will find it very beneficial to have a prayer partner who understands these principles and can help you pray through your issues. The Lord has designed His body, the Church, to have many members and to need one another, so it is important for you to be committed to a fellowship of believers and to be in close relationship with other Christians of the same sex. Pray for the Lord to provide you someone who can pray with you as you begin seeking victory in your personal life issues.

If you have experienced much abuse and trauma in your life, you may need to seek regular prayer ministry from a mature, experienced prayer partner to help you begin this wonderful journey. However, you can rest assured that the Lord is able to set you free as long as you are willing to take each step with Him at your side. Find yourself a prayer partner, give him or her a copy of this book to study with you, become a part of a prayer group that is designed to train believers in this type of prayer, and then pray for the Lord to give you the courage and strength to face your deepest emotional struggles with the Lord.

Those readers who are unbelievers, and those who are unsure about your salvation can experience the Lord's wonderful healing as well, if you are willing to pray with a Christian friend. Jesus said, "He causes His sun to rise on the evil and the good, and sends rain on the righteous and the unrighteous" (Matthew

5:45). This means that God does good even for those who reject Him and do not know Him. He wants you to experience His peace as well, but He is even more concerned about your eternal peace. The Scriptures say He "desires all men to be saved and to come to the knowledge of the truth" (1 Timothy 2:4) and He wants you to come into His family so that you can live with Him eternally. If you are willing to pray with a Christian prayer partner you can replace the pain in your life with God's peace as well. My prayer for you is that this will lead you to desire to know Him in a personal way so that He can be your constant companion and counselor.

If you want to know Jesus as your Savior and have eternal life, you are encouraged to seek the guidance of a strong Christian friend or pastor to explain this simple process to you. Or you can do it anywhere by understanding the following four principles.

First, understand that God loves you and wants you to spend eternity with Him. The Bible says that He "desires all men to be saved and to come to the knowledge of the truth" (1 Timothy 2:4). Second, realize that you have sinned and fallen short of God's standards. Romans 3:23 tells us that "all have sinned and fall short of the glory of God." Third, understand that Jesus was the sinless Son of God and when He died, He paid the penalty for your sins. Romans 5:8 tells us that "God demonstrates His own love toward us, in that while we were yet sinners, Christ died for us." And finally, understand that you cannot live a life that's good enough to go to heaven, but since Jesus paid the penalty for your sins you can be forgiven and go to heaven by accepting Jesus as your Savior, as a gift from God. Ephesians 2:8-9 says, "For by grace you have been saved through faith; and that not of yourselves, it is the gift of God; not as a result of works, that no one should boast." If you understand these four simple principles and want to have a personal relationship with Jesus, you may find it helpful to say the following prayer or simply speak to God with similar words. It's not the words you say that are so important as the attitude in your heart.

Suggested Prayer:*Lord Jesus, I come to you now, confessing that I am a sinner and that I need your forgiveness. Thank you for loving me and dying for my sins. I ask you to forgive me for all my sins and I accept your forgiveness and salvation as a free gift. I invite you now to come into my heart and to be my Savior. I pray this in Jesus' name, Amen.*

If you just prayed this prayer sincerely, you can rest assured that all your sins have been forgiven and you are now a child of God. It is critical that you find a good fellowship of Christians who can help you in your new life with God and teach you how to walk in the power of the Holy Spirit. May God bless you as you enter into this new, wonderful life. You are not alone; the Lord will be your constant companion, Comforter, guide, and friend and He has promised that He will never leave you or forsake you (Hebrews 13:5).

CHAPTER 1

Emotions: Friends or Foes?

I was visiting with a young woman during her first counseling session and gathering information to understand the problems she was experiencing. This young lady had grown up in a military family and she carried herself in a very dignified way. Her four children sat quietly in the waiting room like little soldiers and behaved perfectly during the hour-long session. It was clear that she was a good mother and a strong Christian.

She described how her husband treated her and had on numerous occasions yelled at her or treated her disrespectfully in front of their children so I asked her, "How did that make you feel?" She responded by telling me that she thought it was inappropriate behavior, so I asked her again how it made her feel. She told me that she thought it could cause the children to lose their respect for her eventually. I agreed that her husband's behavior sounded disrespectful and was not a good example for their children but I was wanting to know what emotions she felt when her husband treated her in this manner. She finally stated, "It made me feel bad. I guess I felt somewhat angry and insulted."

She went on to explain that her husband often treated her in such a manner so I asked her to give me another example. She said that one day she was working on the computer and her husband told her to turn off the computer because it was bothering him while he was watching a television program. She told him that she would turn it off in a minute but he immediately walked over to the computer and unplugged it and returned to the couch to watch his television program. I asked her again, "How did that make you feel?" She stated that she thought it was rude and inappropriate for him to treat her that way. Since she had not answered my question I asked her again, "How did that make you feel? What emotions do you feel right now as you describe that incident?" She was obviously disturbed by this question and said, "Why are you so focused on my feelings? I've always been taught that as Christians we need to stand firm on our beliefs and not allow our emotions to control us, but you seem to be most concerned about my feelings. Why is that?"

"I agree that it is important to learn to stand firmly on what we know to be the truth," I answered, "but I have also learned that our feelings are very important to understand for a number of reasons. First, because our emotions expose the beliefs we have that are causing us to feel badly. Secondly, negative feelings are what lead people to seek counseling. If they have no negative feelings they would never seek help from others; so I want to understand how they feel. I can't help them feel better unless I understand clearly how they are feeling." I also suggested to this young lady that many Christians have been taught that feelings are bad, so they have learned to suppress them, which eventually leads to an emotional outburst or to some undesired behavior. The truth is that our feelings are very important to God as well.

Emotions are Important to God

You maybe surprised, like this young woman, to know that your emotions are very important to the Lord. In John 14:1 and 27 the apostle John records for us the words the Lord Jesus spoke to His disciples twice on the night of His betrayal. He said to them, "Let not your heart be troubled, nor let it be fearful." The emotions of the disciples were apparently very important to Jesus because He repeatedly comforted them the night before He was betrayed and told them that He wanted them to experience His peace. The Lord also spoke of His peace in John 16:33 when He said to the disciples, "These things I have spoken to you, that in Me you may have peace. In the world you have tribulation, but take courage; I have overcome the world." Clearly, the Lord was concerned about their feelings of discouragement, fear and sadness, and He wanted them to be at peace.

The apostle Paul also understood the importance of feelings. He expressed at the beginning of each of his letters the desire that the believers would have the "peace of God" in their hearts, and spoke of God's peace frequently. Every book of the New Testament except for one contains statements expressing the desirability of believers having peace in their hearts, or speaking of God as the "God of peace."

We're also told by Paul in Galatians 5:22 that the first three fruits, or evidences, of having the Holy Spirit working in our lives are love, joy, and peace, which are all emotions. As we grow in spiritual maturity we will experience these emotions more and more, regardless of the circumstances we find ourselves in. And that is why Paul ended his second letter to the Thessalonians by saying, "Now may the Lord of peace Himself continually grant you peace in every circumstance" (3:16).

Our emotions are important to God, and wise pastors and church leaders realize how important our feelings are, too. One mature pastor I know regularly expresses his desire that those attending his services will leave the church service with a good feeling in their heart. The truth is that if the members of a church do not feel good most of the time when they leave the services of the church, they will eventually leave that church. If they feel wanted, accepted, noticed, encouraged, and blessed to have attended the services they are likely to return. This does not mean that every service has to be encouraging, but there should be more encouraging sermons than condemning ones that make the attendees feel badly. There are many topics that must be addressed from the pulpit that may not be comfortable to the congregation, but when they are placed in the context of the love, grace, and mercy of God they can be encouraging still. The important point here is that our feelings are, indeed, important to God, and should be to each of us as well.

Psalms: The Book of Emotions

David often expressed strong feelings in the book of Psalms and modeled for us how to deal with difficult circumstances and strong feelings. He did not suppress his emotions like most Christians do today; he expressed them to the Lord. I remember as a young Christian that I avoided the book of Psalms and thought the Psalms were discouraging because David was always complaining about his enemies and crying out to God for help. But now, forty years later, I love the Psalms and find them comforting in times of difficulties when I am feeling similar emotions to those expressed in them.

Many of the Psalms are Psalms of praise and worship of the Lord, but many of them are Psalms of distress and despair. David was a man who was "in touch" with his feelings. He did not suppress them and stuff them inside like so many do today. He cried out to the Lord when he was distressed, when he was overwhelmed, when he was fearful, when he was lonely, and when he felt guilty and ashamed; and he repeatedly made statements such as, "I will cry to God Most High, To God who accomplishes all things for me" (Psalm 57:2). I believe that one of the most significant contributions of the book of Psalms is that it gives us a deeply personal look into the thoughts and feelings of a godly man, and shows us how we should deal with our feelings as well.

The book of Psalms is rich and full of truth and wisdom for us, also. But there are many valuable and unique lessons we can learn from Psalms, including the way we as believers should handle our emotions. We should learn to talk with the Lord about our emotions, cry out to Him for His help, express our feelings openly, make our requests known to God, commit our ways and our lives to the Lord, and then trust Him to do whatever is in His perfect will. Whatever else we may learn from Psalms, we should certainly learn that God wants to hear our cry and our emotions, and He is able to provide us the strength, comfort, and emotional relief we need. In Psalm 23:2-3 David wrote, "He makes me lie down in green pastures; He leads me beside quiet waters. He restores my soul." God wants us to learn to find emotional peace and rest, and He wants to restore our souls when we are emotionally distraught for any reason.

The Lord Jesus Had Strong Emotions

The Scriptures tell us that the Lord Jesus also had strong emotions at times. In Hebrews 5:7 we're told that, "In the days of His flesh, He offered up both prayers and supplications with loud crying and tears." "Loud crying and tears" means that He had very strong feelings and He was not ashamed to express them. It is because of His earthly walk and experiences that we can have confidence that He understands our feelings when we are suffering emotionally. Hebrews 4:15-16 tells us, "we do not have a high priest who cannot sympathize with our weaknesses, but One who has been tempted in all things as we are, yet without sin. Let us therefore draw near with confidence to the throne of grace, that we may receive mercy and may find grace to help in time of need."

The Lord Jesus experienced many strong emotions during His thirty-three years of life on this earth. The main difference between His experience and ours was that His emotions never led Him to sin, whereas ours will if we do not learn how to deal with them. James 1:14-15 tells us that "...each one is tempted when he is carried away and enticed by his own lust [strong emotions]. Then when lust [strong emotions] has conceived, it gives birth to sin; and when sin is accomplished, it brings forth death." The word that is usually translated as "lust" in this passage means literally "strong emotions," so this passage teaches us that our emotions will lead us into sinful behavior if we do not learn how to deal with them.

Another important difference between the Lord's emotions and ours is that His emotions were always based on the truth, whereas our emotions are often based on lies and misinterpretations that we have of events in our lives. The Lord Jesus did not believe any misinterpretations because He was "full of grace and truth" (John 1:14) and He was "the way, and the truth, and the life" (John 14:6). He had no falsehoods in His mind to cause Him to feel bad unnecessarily, whereas our minds are full of lies, falsehoods, and misinterpretations that lead us to many wrong conclusions and negative feelings. That's why the apostle Paul instructs us in Philippians 4:8 to let our minds dwell on "whatever is true," and he states in the following verse that the result of doing this will be that "the God of peace shall be with you."

Emotions that Jesus Did Not Experience

Although Jesus experienced many painful emotions and understands our feelings, there are also many emotions He never experienced which we do, because many of our emotions are based upon distorted beliefs we have, and the Lord did not have any distorted beliefs. Guilt is a good example of an emotion that Jesus did not experience, because He never sinned and never felt feelings of shame or guilt. However, He did experience strong feelings of truth-based dread, fact-based anger, disappointment, sadness, and grief, which we will examine in later chapters.

Fear is another emotion that Jesus never experienced. He repeatedly told His disciples not to fear, and the apostle John learned this so well that he wrote, "perfect love casts out fear" (1 John 4:18). The antidote to fear is having a firm belief that God is with you at all times, and feeling His presence. When this exists, there is no fear. Other emotions that fit into this category of belief-based emotions (emotions based on false beliefs) include aloneness, helplessness, hopelessness, shame, defilement, and hurt. All of these emotions are common human feelings based upon erroneous beliefs we hold, but since Jesus held no erroneous beliefs He never felt these feelings.

The fact that Jesus never experienced the entire range of human emotions does not mean that He is unable to sympathize with our feelings. The negative fact-based feelings that He felt feel the same as the belief-based negative feelings that we feel. There is very little difference in the actual physiological or visceral experiences of our negative feelings, and many times people cannot even distinguish one from another. It takes some effort for many people to articulate their emotions because all of the negative feelings feel "bad." This is the reason why many people can only talk about their feelings in terms of the four generic groups of "mad, sad, glad, and bad." Jesus knows our feelings, and He knows how bad we feel when we feel bad. He empathizes with our bad feelings even when they are belief-based and not truth-based.

The Lord Understands our Feelings

The Lord knows what it feels like to be all alone and rejected. He knows what it feels like to be angry at injustices and evil behavior. He experienced disappointment and sadness at times. And He experienced joy and love at other times. Not only does He understand our feelings, but I believe that sometimes He weeps with us when we are sad because He "sympathizes" with us (Heb. 4:15). In 1 Corinthians 12:26 the apostle Paul told the church that when one member of the church "suffers, all the members suffer with it; if one member is honored, all the members rejoice with it."

One of the most profound verses in the Bible is John 11:35, where we are told that "Jesus wept." What an amazing thing it is that the Son of God was capable of weeping, even when He knew what the future held and He knew that He was going to resurrect Lazarus in a few minutes to end the grieving of His friends. He saw the sadness of His dear friends, and when Mary fell at His feet weeping out of her deep sorrow, "Jesus wept." John 11: 33 says, "When Jesus therefore saw her weeping, and the Jews who came with her, also weeping, He was deeply moved in spirit, and was troubled."

Many times when people are led to the Lord in prayer in order to deal with the pain they experienced from a childhood trauma, they report visualizations in their mind that are expressive of biblical truths. For example, one woman who had suffered many childhood traumas from being abused by her parents reported that in her memory she was left all alone, abandoned by her family. Then she reported a visualization of the Lord Jesus walking towards her, a visual representation of the biblical truth that she was not really alone. When asked to report if she had any more visualizations she stated that she

visualized the Lord Jesus kneeling down to look her in the face
and she saw tears in His eyes, and He told her that He was sad
about her abuse also. This was a visual representation of the
biblical truth that Jesus understands our feelings and "weep[s]
with those who weep" (Romans 12:15). It is a wonderful comfort
to know that the Lord truly sympathizes with us and empathizes
with our weaknesses and understands how we feel.

Emotions Reveal Our True Beliefs

Once we are saved and know that our sins are forgiven and
we are going to heaven, there is a wonderful transformation
that occurs automatically in many of our beliefs, values, and
behaviors. We generally feel good at the time of salvation also,
but we do not stay on that emotional high for long, and we soon
discover that we continue to have negative experiences and
negative feelings, even after our conversion. In some ways the
life of the believer is more difficult and troubled than the life
of the unbeliever because of the persecution and rejection we
receive from the world, but we have the presence of the Lord
and the comfort of the Holy Spirit to strengthen us.

There are also many areas of the Christian's mind that are
not automatically renewed when a person is converted. That is
why the Scriptures repeatedly exhort believers to be "renewed
in the mind," (Romans 12:2, Ephesians 4:23) because they
continue to be subject to the influence of deeply embedded,
faulty beliefs about themselves. As a result, we experience many
negative emotions that are based upon our faulty beliefs. The
Lord wants to renew our minds at a very deep, basic level.

When our emotions are not fact-based or reality-based, they
are based upon lies we have come to believe, and these beliefs
are sometimes contradicted by our intellectual beliefs. We may,
for example, believe intellectually the Scripture that "my God
shall supply all [my] needs" (Philippians 4:19) but our deepest
beliefs, the ones that control our feelings, will be exposed when
we lose our job and have difficulty finding another one. You
may intellectually believe that God will take care of you, but
you may find yourself feeling very anxious and uncertain that

it will actually happen. Your true beliefs are those that control your emotions and your behaviors.

The early Christians believed that God could deliver Peter from prison and were praying fervently for his release (Acts 12:5) but they also knew that God had allowed Stephen to be stoned and James to be beheaded. When God answered their prayers and supernaturally released Peter, Peter went to their place of prayer and knocked at the door, but they did not really believe he was going to be delivered, so they continued praying after the servant girl told them that he was standing at the door. Their true belief that God would not hear their prayer was exposed.

Peter later wrote in his first epistle, "you have been distressed by various trials, that the proof of your faith, being more precious than gold which is perishable, even though tested by fire, may be found to result in praise and glory and honor" (1 Peter 1:6-7). What he was saying in this passage was that the trials we experience reveal the purity of our beliefs, and expose the lies we believe so that they can be removed, in the same way that heating gold until it melts allows the goldsmith to remove the impurities as they are revealed when they rise to the top, and can then be skimmed off. Our feelings, when they are lie-based, expose our false beliefs so that we can seek to have the Lord remove the lies and give us peace. This is the way the Lord renews our minds. At salvation, our hearts were renewed, but our minds are in need of continuing renewal until we are taken home to be with the Lord.

Emotions Were Created by God and Are Good

Practically everything we do and every decision we make is based upon our feelings and our desires to feel good. Sometimes we must do things that do not make us feel good and this is where self-control becomes important, but the reality is that most of the time our actions and decisions are based upon our feelings.

We may protest this and wish that we had no feelings because they tend to lead us astray, but God is the One Who created us and gave us these emotions. This is part of what it means to be "made in the image of God." God has emotions, and He created us like Him so that we have emotions also. If we had no negative emotions we would have no positive emotions either, because they come from the same source. When we suppress our emotions completely and numb ourselves, we also lose our ability to love others and to enjoy life.

No, God created our feelings and He has given us the means to deal with our negative emotions and to experience love, joy, and peace. Feelings are good, and one day we who are believers and who have received Him as our Savior will experience joys that are inconceivable to us now. And in that day, we are told in Revelation 21:4, "He shall wipe away every tear from their eyes; and there shall no longer be any death; there shall no longer be any mourning, or crying, or pain; the first things have passed away." What a wonderful day that will be!

In the meantime, we have been promised that we have a Comforter, the Holy Spirit, the Wonderful Counselor who is available to help us, and we have the powerful privilege of prayer that can provide us the means for experiencing the "peace of God which surpasses all comprehension," which "shall guard your hearts and your minds in Christ Jesus" (Philippians 4:7). In the coming chapters we will examine how we can experience supernatural relief from our negative emotions through the power of the Holy Spirit and through prayer.

Feelings of Confusion

Many times the people you deal with have suppressed their feelings so long and have such a bundle of different emotions that they don't know how they feel. They are like a large ball of yarn with each strand of yarn representing a different type of emotion, all of which are inter-connected. When asked how they feel they may tell you they feel "confused" and the task of the prayer partner, if someone comes to you for help, may be to help them unravel this ball, one strand at a time, so that they understand why they feel the way they do.

Feelings of confusion can sometimes be removed as the prayer partner encourages the person to talk while he simply listens and helps put words to their feelings. At times, it is helpful to simply begin with these feelings of confusion and pray for the Lord to help sort out the confusion and bring clarity to the person. If you are praying on your own, you might simply pray, "Lord, would you come right now and bring clarity to my mind? What is it that You want me to know right now?" After you say this brief prayer, just listen quietly and see what thoughts come into your mind. Follow these thoughts and begin to unravel the tangled mess of emotions you are feeling until you can identify the dominant feeling. If you cannot do this alone, seek assistance from a mature Christian friend who is willing to pray with you.

It is also very helpful to know that although there are hundreds of feeling words in the English language, most of them can be classified into one of the following two types of emotions, and into one of the 12 specific emotions identified, below.

Type I: Grief, Disappointment, Sadness, True Guilt and Justifiable Anger

Type II: Aloneness, False Shame, Defilement, Fear, Hurt, Helplessness and Hopelessness

The remainder of this book is divided into two main sections. The first section will deal with the class of fact-based emotions which include grief, disappointment, sadness, true guilt, and justifiable anger. The second section will deal with the belief-based emotions of fear, loneliness, false shame, hurt, helplessness, hopelessness, and defilement. The Lord is able to remove all of these negative feelings when they are exposed and when we are willing to face them and allow Him to remove them, but the means of their removal depends on whether they are fact-based or belief-based. We will begin with the powerful emotion of grief and see how the Lord is able to set us free from debilitating, painful feelings of grief.

SECTION A

DEALING WITH FACT-BASED EMOTIONS

Prayer Principle 1: 1 Peter 5:7

"Casting all your care upon Him;
for He careth for you."(KJV)

CHAPTER 2

Overcoming Grief and Loss

There is no emotion that demonstrates more clearly the power of Jesus to bring rapid and permanent healing to our emotions than grief and loss. So, I will begin this section of the book by addressing how the Lord helps us in times of grief.

Biblical Examples of Grief and Loss

There are many examples in the Scriptures of grief and loss that illustrate the powerful emotional impact it has, even upon men and women of strong faith. In the New Testament, of course, we have the account of the death of Lazarus of Bethany and the sorrow that it brought to his sisters Mary and Martha. John 11:19 tells us that "many of the Jews had come to Martha and Mary, to console them concerning their brother." Jesus first spoke with Martha and gave her words of encouragement, but Mary, when she came to Jesus, fell at his feet and wept saying, "Lord, if you had been here, my brother would not have died" (v. 32). Her grief was so intense that the Scriptures tell us Jesus "was deeply moved in spirit, and was troubled" (John 11:33).

The Old Testament provides us numerous examples of the power of grief and loss. Even when loved ones die at an old age, according to the normal course of life, their loss can be very painful to their spouse and their children. When Sarah died at the age of 127, Abraham "went in to mourn for Sarah and to weep for her" (Genesis 23:2). He bought a burial site for her

in the land of Canaan and buried her there. But his son Isaac
continued to grieve for his mother until he took Rebekah to be
his wife, and the Scriptures tell us that "he loved her; thus Isaac
was comforted after his mother's death" (Genesis 24:67).

It is normal for parents to die before their children, but
when children die before their parents this is extremely painful
for the parents who nurtured them and cared for them all their
lives and expected to see them grow up and live beyond their
own lifespan. After Jacob's sons sold their brother Joseph into
slavery and reported to their father that he had been killed by a
wild animal, Jacob mourned deeply for Joseph. The Scriptures
tell us that "Jacob tore his clothes, and put sackcloth on his loins,
and mourned for his son many days. Then all his sons and all his
daughters arose to comfort him, but he refused to be comforted.
And he said, 'Surely I will go down to Sheol in mourning for my
son.' So his father wept for him." (Genesis 37:34-35) Of course,
Joseph was not really dead and eventually was reunited with his
father, but Jacob believed he was dead and mourned a long time
for him.

We see the same reaction from King David who was
described as a "man after His [God's] own heart" (1 Samuel
13:14). David was a man of strong faith who was known for his
mighty acts of valor, and yet he was broken and devastated by
the loss of his son Absalom who had attempted to assassinate
him and dethrone him. Listen to the anguish in his soul as he
cried out in 2 Samuel 18:33, "O my son Absalom, my son, my
son Absalom! Would I had died instead of you, O Absalom, my
son, my son!" Even though his troops had won a great victory
and saved the kingdom from being torn from him, David would
not be comforted. "And the king covered his face and cried out
with a loud voice, 'O my son Absalom, O Absalom, my son, my
son!'" (2 Samuel 19:4) Many people who have lost their children
can empathize with the pain that David felt for his son, even
though he was a rebellious son who had done much evil.

The depth of pain that is felt differs greatly from individual
to individual depending upon the nature of their relationship
with the deceased person, the circumstances of their death, and

the overall impact their death has upon the surviving person. A child who is an independent adult and who loses a parent who is elderly and sickly is likely to grieve far less than a child who is still dependent upon his parent and loses his only caregiver. The impact of the loss is far greater and the depth of the emotion felt by that child is likely to be far greater.

Facts about Grief and Loss

Grief is normal. Regardless of the circumstance behind a loss, grief is a normal reaction to the loss of a loved one. My mother-in-law came to live with us the last several years of her life due to declining health and her diminishing ability to care for herself. I had never been really close to her or had much opportunity to talk with her and spend time with her, and while she lived with us it was difficult to carry on meaningful conversations with her. She had numerous strokes and during the last few weeks of her life she lay in her bed unable to communicate at all and slowly deteriorating.

One night as we were turning her over in her bed I saw that her eyes were rolled up and she looked as if she were dead, and a pang of sadness and grief suddenly struck my heart as I recognized the signs of imminent death and knew she probably would not live through the night. I spent some time at her bedside and prayed and tried to speak with her, but there was no response. When I woke early the next morning I went immediately to her bedside to check on her, and she was gone. I began to weep over her. The magnitude of my grief surprised me since I had never been particularly close to her, but I wept intensely to the point that I could barely talk to inform her children that she had died. Sometimes grief is very profound, and sometimes it is more like sadness, depending upon many factors, but it is not a sign of weakness or lack of faith.

Grief can be deeply painful. A young couple came to me who had been married a very short time. They were both working, trying to build their life of dreams and were excited when they learned that the wife was pregnant with her first child. Near the end of her pregnancy they closed on a house and worked to make it ready for their child. The young woman had no problems with her pregnancy and delivered the child then took it to their home while the husband continued preparing their new home for his wife and newborn child. Two weeks later the house was ready and the couple moved into their new home with the child. Sometime in the middle of the night the wife went to check on the child and found it lying motionless in its crib, not breathing. She frantically called for her husband and tried to give it CPR but it was too late. They lost their little, sweet infant on the first night they spent in their new home.

This loss was so devastating and so traumatic that neither of them was able to return to their jobs. They could not stand to go inside their new home anymore because of the traumatic memory and were living with the wife's parents at the time. They could not sleep or resume life and after several weeks of this went to a mental health clinic for help. As they sat in my office they were so distraught that they could not tolerate talking about it or working to find emotional resolution. They simply wanted some immediate relief and wanted to speak with a psychiatrist and receive some medications to help them relax and get some sleep. They were in a deep state of pain that was completely debilitating to them.

Grief can result from many kinds of losses. Grief can result not simply from the death of a loved one but from many kinds of losses. Sometimes it results from the loss of a parent who abandons the family, leaving the child without a father or mother. Or a spouse may experience strong feelings of grief when his/her partner divorces him/her and leaves. At other times it may result from a child's loss of his/her intact family when his/her parents divorce or separate. It may even occur when an accident occurs that leads to a disability and the loss of financial stability. Some children suffer significantly when their family moves frequently or moves at a sensitive time in their life when they need the security of stable friends in their lives. When a child loses all his friends and has to establish new friendships, there may be feelings of grief that need resolution. One young man trained for years to become a professional pianist and then developed a severe case of tendonitis that ended his musical dreams and forced him to develop another career plan. Sometimes professional athletes suffer injuries or medical conditions that abruptly end their careers and this sudden loss of dreams and physical abilities is a very significant loss that triggers off grief reactions. Many kinds of losses can lead to grief reactions.

Grief can have debilitating effects in our lives. I have had the opportunity to counsel many adolescents, and have been amazed to find that over half of the troubled teenagers I have seen have substantial grief and loss issues that contribute significantly to their problem behaviors. Many young people are unable to articulate their feelings or explain why they get into trouble and begin using drugs, but my experience has led me to believe that many of them have unresolved grief issues in their lives that made them feel badly and led them to get into fights, use illegal drugs, and engage in antisocial activities in order to feel better.

Many adults also experience debilitating effects from unresolved grief. One morning I was eating breakfast and reading at a fast-food restaurant and I began talking with a gentleman who was sitting nearby. Shortly into our conversation I learned that he was homeless, and I asked him about his family and where he was from. He informed me that he was originally from California and had only become homeless the last two years after his mother died, when he became depressed and lost all motivation in his life. I asked him if he still felt sadness and pain when he thought about his mother and he said he did, so I then asked him if he would like to get rid of that pain if he could. He stated that he would like that, and so I led him through some prayers and showed him how to give those feelings to the Lord. When we were finished I asked him how he felt about the loss of his mother now, and he thought about it for a few moments and said that he felt fine now, and no longer felt that pain in his chest. As he left the restaurant he informed me of his intention to go back to California and resume his life and his vocation which he had abandoned two years earlier.

Grief does not have to last for years. King Solomon tells us in Ecclesiastes 3:4, there is "A time to weep, and a time to laugh;

a time to mourn, and a time to dance." Mourning does not have to last forever, and the Lord is able to lift it from us and carry it for us. Psalm 30:5 says that "weeping may endure for a night, but joy cometh in the morning" (KJV). Although grief is a normal reaction, it is not the Lord's intention that we remain in mourning for the rest of our lives. He wants to replace it with His peace, so that it does not become debilitating in our lives and impede His plans for us.

Some individuals do not experience deep grief in their lives when they lose a loved one, in spite of their deep love for the individual. They may even be relieved at a death when the loved one has suffered great pain, or when they had become completely disabled. An elderly man died and his wife still had many of her children living close by to assist her. At the funeral she asked me if she was going to have to go through the stages of grief, and I told her that it wasn't necessary because it doesn't happen to all people. A year later she thanked me for telling her this, because she was experiencing peace in her life, and she knew she did not have to feel guilty about not carrying grief over the loss of her husband. Although she was very close to him and had a good relationship with him, she never experienced strong feelings of grief over her husband.

Caring friends can be comforting to grieving individuals. John 11:19 tells us that "many of the Jews had come to Martha and Mary, to console them concerning their brother." All throughout the Scriptures it can be seen that family members and friends are able to provide comfort to those who are grieving, and this strong tradition can be observed in virtually all cultures. In my own personal experience I found this to be true. When my father died it was very comforting to see friends who loved him and cared for him come to his funeral. These were people who could share my sorrow and understand my grief because they also were grieving for him. One particular man who was a close friend of my father came to the funeral, and when he arrived at the funeral home it was a wonderful feeling to know that he cared enough to drive a long distance from another state to be present at the funeral. His familiar smile was a comfort.

When this gentleman turned to view my father's body, his face contorted in grief and he turned away to weep. That response told me that he was grieving also, and that he loved my father and missed him, and it was very comforting to have him present at that time. Family friends are very important to have around in times of grief and can provide much comfort.

Grief can be complicated by other factors and feelings. Grief is sometimes complicated by other factors and emotions that can cause it to be prolonged. A friend's 40-year-old husband had a stroke while he was golfing one day, and then he suffered a heart attack. He remained in a coma for months but did survive, although he was brain damaged and completely disabled, requiring care in a nursing home for three years. When he eventually died this woman grieved over his loss, but she had already lost him, for all practical purposes, three years earlier. She had had to adjust to living alone without his help, having to spend all of her spare time visiting him in the nursing home, and trying to take care of their finances and her home by herself. When her husband finally died, she then had to adjust to being all alone without the support of her husband's family, and she had to deal with a lack of meaningful social relationships. As other male friends began to show her attention, she had to deal with the insecurity of dating again, and experiencing feelings of rejection and aloneness that she had not experienced since her adolescent years. All of these factors complicated her life and her grief reactions to the loss of her husband. Sometimes individuals deal with unresolved feelings of anger or guilt about the deceased person, and this also can complicate their grieving and prolong their period of loss.

The Lord is able to release us from our grief. When I began counseling adolescent boys in group homes several years ago, a 17-year-old boy was admitted into the program who had lost his best friend only three weeks earlier. When I first met him it was obvious that he was still in a great deal of emotional pain from this loss. He had been living with his cousin who was his best friend. When the cousin went to buy some drugs from his dealer, the dealer, who was strung out on drugs, thought the cousin had come to rob him, and shot and killed him. The young man in my office stated that he had hardly slept in the last three weeks and he was worn out. I asked him if he would like to get rid of that pain if he could, and he said that he would do anything to get rid of it. With his permission, I prayed with him about his loss and led him in a prayer in which he gave these feelings to the Lord and asked Him to carry them for him. We also revisited an earlier grief memory that had implanted some false guilt in him, and the Lord brought the truth to his mind that it was not his fault. When we were finished 40 minutes later I asked him to think about his cousin and tell me how he felt. To his surprise he found that he no longer had any pain, but felt peaceful about his cousin.

The next day I saw this young man outdoors mowing the lawn, and I approached him and asked him how he was doing. He stated that he had slept well the previous night for the first time in three weeks. I asked him if he had been thinking any more about his cousin and he smiled and said, "Yes, but I'm just remembering the good times we had together. I don't feel any pain anymore." I continued to meet with him for the next five months to follow up with him, and those feelings of grief never returned. He had other emotional issues to deal with from time to time, but those painful feelings of grief were resolved. The Lord removed his grief completely through the prayers we said together.

This is not an isolated case of one individual who had a dramatic recovery from traumatic grief. I have seen the Lord suddenly and dramatically remove grief from individuals in numerous cases, sometimes after years of unresolved grief. A middle-aged woman was seen for an evaluation one time and in the process of collecting background information on her I learned that she had been raised by her maternal grandmother. The mere mention of this grandmother caused this woman to break down in tears even though her death had occurred twelve years earlier. I asked her if she would like to get rid of those painful feelings of grief if possible and she stated that she would, so I prayed with her and saw those feelings lifted in a matter of a few minutes. When I asked her to try to make herself feel those painful feelings again, she was unable to do so.

Grief is a normal feeling to the loss of a significant relationship and it can be deeply painful. But the Lord does not desire us to live with it indefinitely or to be debilitated by it for even a few months. The Lord Jesus comforted His disciples but did not rebuke them for their sadness and grief at His announcement that He was leaving them. He stated in John 16:20-22, "Truly, truly, I say to you, that you will weep and lament, but the world will rejoice; you will be sorrowful, but your sorrow will be turned to joy. Whenever a woman is in travail she has sorrow, because her hour has come; but when she gives birth to the child, she remembers the anguish no more, for joy that a child has been born into the world. Therefore, you too now have sorrow; but I will see you again, and your heart will rejoice, and no one takes your joy away from you."

Symptoms of Unresolved Grief

We're going to look at how the Lord is able to take away our grief, but first let's talk about the symptoms of unresolved grief. How can you tell if you have unresolved grief? What are the symptoms of unresolved grief?

1. *Sleep difficulties.* The 17-year-old boy struggled with sleeplessness that was caused by thinking obsessively about his cousin at night when he was trying to sleep. If you are unable to sleep sufficiently due to thinking about a deceased person, if you are frequently awakened by intrusive dreams about a deceased person, or you wake up in the middle of the night and cannot fall back asleep due to thinking about the loss of a loved one, then you probably have unresolved grief.

2. *Thoughts about the deceased trigger tears.* I did an evaluation on a woman one time and in the process of conducting the interview I inquired about her family. She had been raised by her grandmother, and when she began to talk about her, she broke down and began crying profusely and talking about how much

she still missed her after her death 12 years earlier. Her grandmother had been like a mother to her and raised her, and the mere mention of her name evoked strong emotions of sadness and grief. I asked her if she would like to get rid of this pain if she could, and she said she would, so I led her in some prayers and the Lord lifted the pain from her within a few minutes.

3. *Deep pain in the chest when reminded about the deceased.*
A young pastor and his wife who lost their first-born daughter did not cry when they thought about their daughter, but did feel strong feelings of pain in their chests when reminded of her. After years of carrying this pain they were able to release all that pain and give it to the Lord through prayer. Today they can talk about her and may feel a small sadness but not the overwhelming pain they previously had.

4. *Depression.* A strong Christian man lost one of his sons to suicide, and then about six years later his wife also committed suicide. He was overwhelmed with grief and sadness and tried praying about it, quoting Scriptures, and dwelling on the truth but he could not overcome his grief. It soon developed into depression and he became overwhelmed with intrusive thoughts of worthlessness and feelings of hopelessness. He went to his doctor, who placed him on antidepressant medications. The negative thoughts persisted until he was hospitalized and given shock treatments to help him feel better. I began seeing him after he was discharged from the hospital, and the depressive thoughts and grief were still there, so I began praying with him about his emotions. The grief was quickly removed through prayers, and then we continued to pray about his feelings of hopelessness and worthlessness until they were completely removed. What medications and shock treatments failed to do, the Lord was able to do as this man simply learned to take all his troubles to the Lord in prayer.

5. *Behavior problems dating back to the loss.* Many of the teenage youth that I have counseled can date their problems back to a significant loss. Some young people begin drinking alcohol and using drugs to feel better after they have lost a loved one. One boy lost his brother, who died of an asthma attack in the middle of the night while they were sleeping. This was traumatic for him, but then a year later he lost his mother also. He began to skip school, drink, and use drugs. He was eventually placed in state custody, but continued to use drugs every opportunity he had, and refused to talk about his grief. After getting drunk, driving illegally, and almost killing himself in a car wreck he finally agreed to talk about his grief and prayed about it. Once he gave his grief to the Lord he began to behave better and was able to stay out of trouble.

The Lord Will Give You Rest

In each of the examples given above these individuals found relief from their grief through prayer and giving their grief and loss to the Wonderful Counselor. The Lord beckons us, "Come unto me, all ye that labour and are heavy laden, and I will give you rest" (Matthew 11:28, KJV). He does not want us to remain in our grief, but wants to take it and carry it for us.

He was acquainted with grief. Isaiah 53:3 speaks of the Lord Jesus and says, "He was despised and forsaken of men; A man of sorrows, and acquainted with grief." What an amazing understatement that is, but what a comfort it is to know that He was "acquainted with grief." During His earthly walk we know that He experienced grief several times. When John the Baptist was beheaded and Jesus was informed about it, "He withdrew from there in a boat, to a lonely place by Himself; and when the multitudes heard of this, they followed Him on foot from the cities" (Matthew 14:13). Jesus ministered to the multitudes and fed the 5,000, but then He sent the multitudes away and made his disciples get into a boat and go ahead of Him to the other side of the sea. Matthew 14:23 says, "And after He had sent them away, He went up to the mountain by Himself to pray." Jesus needed time alone to pray and grieve over the death of his cousin, John the Baptist.

Likewise, in John 11 when his friend Lazarus of Bethany died, we see how the Lord experienced grief over his death, even though He knew He was going to raise him from the dead. When Mary fell at His feet and wept, Jesus "was deeply moved in spirit and was troubled" (John 11:33). And when He was led to the gravesite, the Scriptures tell us that "Jesus wept." What an incredible, compelling thing to consider, that the Son of God felt such sadness and grief that He wept! Jesus truly was "acquainted with grief" as the prophet Isaiah stated.

He empathizes with us in our grief. Not only was Jesus "acquainted with grief," but He also empathizes with us in our grief and weeps with us. With Martha He gave some words of comfort, but with Mary who fell at His feel and wept, He wept with her because He empathized with her feelings. The writer of Hebrews put it this way, "For we do not have a high priest who cannot sympathize with our weaknesses, but one who has been tempted in all things as we are, yet without sin. Let us therefore draw near with confidence to the throne of grace, that we may receive mercy and may find grace to help in time of need" (Hebrews 4:15-16).

It is very comforting to me to realize that Jesus wept with Mary. There are times in our lives when things happen that make us weep, and I believe that many times the Lord is weeping with us as well. Hebrews 5:7 says, "In the days of His flesh, He offered up both prayers and supplications with loud crying and tears to the One able to save Him from death." This passage is speaking about Jesus, and it tells us that He offered up prayers and supplications with loud crying and tears!

Let me ask you, where does that fit into your theology? Many Christians are very confused about emotions and have a warped theology of emotions that says that any negative emotion they have is a sign of weakness or lack of faith, so they have learned to suppress their feelings. The Lord Jesus prayed "with loud crying and tears," and if He wept like this to the Father, we may also. The problem is that most of us won't allow ourselves to feel these emotions.

There is a word for that in the New Testament. It is the word "kataecho," which comes from the word "echo" (meaning "to hold down or restrain,") and the Greek preposition "kata" (which means "down"). This compound word in the New Testament means to "hold down" or "restrain," and is translated as "suppress" in the New American Standard Version where it appears in Romans 1:18, as Paul tells us that "men suppress the truth in unrighteousness."

Do you know what happens when you "hold down" your negative feelings for a long time, never dealing with them but just suppressing them? You may become tired, angry, or depressed. Some people eventually get to where they cannot even remember the incident that caused those feelings, or feel them at all any more. Some people suppress their feelings for so long that they can't feel any emotions; they just walk around feeling numb because they have numbed their feelings for so long. But the Lord gave us these feelings, and He doesn't want us to just numb them. He wants us to take them to Him, and let Him carry them.

His feelings were all truth-based. Jesus was the Truth and the Life and He believed no lies, so all of His feelings were reality-based and truth-based. This is true for His sadness and grief. In spite of the fact that He experienced no lie-based emotions, He nevertheless did experience a range of negative emotions throughout His life, including not only grief and loss, but sadness, disappointment, and anger. When He and his disciples approached Jerusalem, He wept over Jerusalem out of sadness (Luke 19:41). When He cleared the temple (John 2:13-17) and when He saw the hardness of heart of the Pharisees as He healed the man with the withered hand (Mark 3:5), He felt anger in His heart. After His resurrection He was astounded at the lack of belief of His disciples and He rebuked them, out of feelings of disappointment (Mark 16:10-14).

None of the feelings of Jesus were due to weakness or a lack of faith on His part or due to lies He believed, and most of the time these emotions are truth-based for us as well. Jesus can set us free from each of these as we learn to give them to Him and ask Him to take them from us and carry them for us. Just as the Scriptures tell us that He has "borne our griefs, and carried our sorrows" (Isaiah 53: 4, KJV) so, too, He is willing to bear our sadness, anger, and disappointments. We will examine these other emotions in the chapters that follow.

There are many other emotions that we experience which the Lord never felt because He was full of truth and there were no lies in His mind. For example, we never see the Lord being fearful and anxious. In fact, He taught his followers to not be anxious but to cast all their cares upon Him. Jesus sometimes felt righteously angry at the hardness of heart of the religious leaders, but He never felt hurt by their rejection. He knew what was in the hearts of all men (John 2:24-25) and He did not entrust himself to them. Jesus never felt confused, hopeless, helpless, shameful, or defiled, which are all feelings that we experience at times. These feelings are lie-based emotions, and the Lord is able to set us free from each of them by bringing His truth into the picture. As He brings His truth into these emotions, the truth sets us free from these negative emotions. This will be the subject of later chapters.

He wants to bear our grief and carry our sorrows. Notice how consistently the Scriptures tell us that the Wonderful Counselor desires to carry our sorrows. Psalm 30:5 says, "Weeping may last for the night, but a shout of joy comes in the morning." Isaiah 53:4 (KJV) tells us, "Surely he has borne our griefs, and carried our sorrows." In Matthew 5:4 Jesus said in the Sermon on the Mount, "Blessed are those who mourn, for they shall be comforted." In Matthew 11:28 Jesus said, "Come to Me, all who are weary and heavy-laden, and I will give you rest." And Jesus repeatedly comforted his disciples the night before his crucifixion saying, "Let not your heart be troubled; believe in God, believe also in Me" (John 14:1, 27). Then Peter exhorts us in 1 Peter to continually be "casting all your care upon Him, for He careth for you" (1 Peter 5:7, KJV).

The Lord does not want us to carry grief and sorrow for a long time. He wants to lift this burden from us, and He is able and willing to carry it for us. The process is very simple and just involves acknowledging our grief and asking Him to carry it for us. This is the process that I used with each of the individuals described in this chapter, including the 17-year-old boy whose cousin was killed. To make it very clear I will break it into simple steps as follows.

Steps to Releasing Grief and Sorrow

First, be honest with the Lord and acknowledged the full extent of your pain and sorrow. Tell the Lord how much it hurts and how you miss the person who died (or whatever other loss you are experiencing.) Second, ask the Lord to take those feelings from you and carry them for you as He promised he would. Third, ask the Lord what He wants you to know, and then listen quietly to the "still, small voice of God." Be sure that your thoughts are consistent with the Word of God, and pray with a friend, if necessary, who is knowledgeable of the Scriptures. Fourth, after receiving some healing, think about your loved one and try to stir up the pain again to see if it is still present. Fifth, if there is still some remaining pain in the memory, identify what is painful about it and pray again. If other painful feelings surface, identify them and pray with someone who knows how to pray about belief-based pain (this will be covered in Chapters 6-12) to see all of these feelings removed.

The following is a sample prayer that you might find useful. As you pray this prayer, fill in the blanks with the appropriate name and information. Then afterwards meditate quietly and see what thoughts the Lord might bring to your mind to give you His perfect peace. Once He gives you His peace, take the time to thank Him for what He just did for you.

Dear Lord, as I think about _____ *it fills my heart with pain and grief because I miss him/her so much. I miss many things about him/her, especially* _____ _____ *, and it makes me sad that he/she is no longer with me. But Lord, I'm tired of feeling this grief and pain, so right now I choose to give it to You, and I ask You to please take it from me, and carry it for me, and replace it with Your peace. I also ask that You bring to me any truth that You want me to know right now. I pray this In Jesus' name. Amen*

CHAPTER 3

Eliminating Anger and Resentment

One morning when I was about fifteen years old I remember going to the breakfast table and finding my father and two of my sisters sitting there quietly and not eating. When I sat down I wondered what was wrong, why they were just sitting there and not eating. And then my father said to me, "Isn't the Lord wonderful?" I sat there awkwardly, knowing the answer but not feeling comfortable saying it because I knew in my head that the Lord was wonderful but I didn't feel it in my heart yet. And so I didn't want to say something that I didn't fully believe in my heart. As my brother and sisters arrived he asked each of them the same question until we were all sitting there awkwardly in silence. My father loved the Lord and just wanted to know that one of his children loved the Lord the same way as he did. He was disappointed that we did not appreciate the Lord the same way that he did. We had an intellectual understanding of the Lord, but we did not yet have an experiential knowledge of the Lord.

There are two ways that you can know someone or something: intellectually and experientially. I was saved at age nine and knew a few things about the Lord, but it took many years for me to come to really know Him experientially. Now that I have come to know Him experientially I can say with conviction that the Lord is wonderful. And in the last five years I have seen Him bring emotional healing to myself and others so often that I can also call Him my "Wonderful Counselor."

He is "wonderful" because He is available to help each of us in times of difficulty, and He wants to give us His incredible peace in every circumstance we face.

In the last chapter we discussed how the Lord helps us in times of grief and loss, and how He is able to supernaturally set us free from the deep pain of losing someone we love. There is hardly a week that goes by when I don't meet someone who is suffering from unresolved grief, who needs comfort. This week, as I was writing this chapter, I prayed with a young person who recently lost his mother and was suffering from deep grief and loss, and I was able to pray with him and see the Lord completely lift this burden and give him peace.

My purpose in writing this book is not to talk about my experience and how I can help you, but to lead you to a close encounter with the Wonderful Counselor. And in this chapter I want to focus on how He can set us free from the grip of anger and resentment. Imagine what a change it would make if the Lord set each one of us completely free from all our grief and anger that we carry inside. Think of the amazing difference it would make in our churches if these two emotions were completely removed from the lives of our church members. Imagine what a difference it would make in a city or county if everyone there were to remove all of their anger and their grief. It would completely transform our society.

Fact-based Anger

"Joey" was a young man whom I had seen several times but who had never really had any urgent issues to discuss. He usually came to my office and we would talk about his week and he would tell me that everything was going well. But this time was different. He told me that he wasn't doing so well; he had been getting into trouble. He almost got into a fight with another boy who said something that made him mad and an adult had to separate them. He stewed in anger for about thirty minutes afterward before he could cool down and be civil with the other boy. Then a few days later he got upset at an adult when he didn't get something he thought he deserved, and he could feel the anger building up inside. I asked Joey, "If you could get rid of that anger completely, would you want to do that?" I ask that question a lot because even the Lord asked people if they wanted to get well. The lame man who had been lame for 38 years was lying at the pool of Bethesda when Jesus walked by and Jesus said to him, "Do you wish to get well?" (John 5:6). Sometimes people don't want to be well and don't want to give up their anger and their pain, so I always ask. And this young man said he would like to get rid of his anger.

I asked Joey how long he had been angry and when he first remembered being so angry, and he told me the first time he remembered getting really angry was when he was seven years old and his mother, who had raised him from birth, drove him and his brother to their father's house and dropped them off. She said that she had to go to the store to buy some cigarettes and she'd be right back. She never returned for them and these boys never saw their mother again. He said he was mad at her for a year and a half and he began to get into fights. Eventually, he began using all kinds of illegal drugs, and began stealing cars. He was full of anger and it was beginning to come out again. Little things that happened would trigger it off and he would blow up and overreact. He said that he hated his mother and never wanted to see her again.

I told Joey that he had a right to be angry and it was okay to be angry at his mother because what she did was wrong, but if he chose to stay angry it would continue to affect him the rest of his life. He said that he didn't want to stay angry and he'd like to get rid of it, so with his permission I prayed with him and gave that anger to the Lord and asked the Lord to carry it for him. The Lord took his anger that moment and set his heart free. At the end of our prayer session he stated that his mother had recently tried to contact him, and that he would like to see her again and get to know her. The anger and hatred he had felt a few minutes earlier was now gone. When he went home that weekend he shocked his father when he told him that he would like to meet his mother, and his father agreed to contact her and try to set up the visit.

Anger is a powerful emotion that can destroy our lives, but the Lord is able to release us from its grips, and He wants to do for each of us what He did for this young man. And for Jesus it is a very simple thing to lift it from us and carry it for us so that we're free of our anger.

The Righteous Anger of Jesus

Not all anger is wrong. King Solomon tells us in Ecclesiastes 3:1, 4 and 8 "There is a time for everything under heaven.... A time to weep, and a time to laugh...A time to love, and a time to hate." Just as I told that young man, it's okay to be angry at times when something bad happens. It was okay for this boy to angry at his mother for abandoning him at such a young age because it was wrong for his mother to do that, regardless of her reasons for doing it. I am sure that she did have a reason for it. She was probably stressed at having to raise the children on her own, and worried about their finances and about feeding and clothing her children. Having to work full-time and discipline children as a single parent is very difficult, but to take the two boys and just drop them off without any warning or explanation was wrong. This boy had a right to be angry.

Even the Lord Jesus was angry at times. A very familiar story is told in John 2:13-17, about the time when Jesus cleared the Temple. He entered and found the money-changers there robbing poor people of their money and using the house of God for personal gain, and it filled Him with righteous anger. He took some cords and wove them together, and then went into that temple and began driving the money-changers out. He overturned their tables and poured out their coins on the floor and shouted at them to "stop making My Father's house a house of merchandise." Jesus had a righteous anger at them because they had turned the house of God into a "den of thieves" (Matthew 21:13, KJV). His anger was justified because it was anger at sin, it was truth-based anger, and it was not out of control.

Another time Jesus became angry was when He came upon a man in a synagogue with a withered hand, and He felt compassion for this man and was about to heal him. But as He looked around He saw the religious leaders watching Him to see if He would heal this man on the Sabbath. They were looking for an opportunity to be able to accuse Him, and they didn't care that this man could be relieved of his suffering or that they would witness a miracle take place. Jesus saw the hardness of their hearts, and Mark 3:5 tells us, "And after looking around at them with anger, grieved at their hardness of heart, He said to the man, 'Stretch out your hand.' And he stretched it out, and his hand was restored." Jesus was righteously angry at these leaders for the hardness of their hearts toward this needy man.

It's okay to be angry at times. All throughout the Scriptures we read about how the wrath of God is revealed from heaven against the unrighteousness of men. Psalm 30:5 tells us that "His anger is but for a moment...but a shout of joy comes in the morning." The anger of Jesus was always truth-based and always under control. Not only was His anger truth-based, but all of His emotions were truth-based.

The Anger of Man

The young man I described earlier had a right to be angry at his mother because she did something terribly wrong. When we hear about parents who abuse their children or about a man abducting a child and then molesting it and murdering it, it should anger us. This is a righteous anger that should both sadden us and anger us.

On September 11, 2001 when the terrorists flew those jets into the Twin Towers in New York City, I remember feeling a number of emotions myself, one of which was anger at the senseless killing of unarmed, innocent civilians by a hateful group of men. War is ugly and bad, but this was not an attack on military targets but on civilians, and the anger felt by thousands was a legitimate anger. Legitimate anger is anger that is based upon an accurate assessment of some evil action rather than a misunderstanding. Sometimes we become angry due to misunderstandings and misinterpretations of events. We have all had individuals who became angry at us because they thought we said something critical of them when we were, in fact, giving them a compliment or when we just chose the wrong words. Truth-based, righteous anger is the only kind of anger that Jesus had, but much of the anger of men is based upon their wrong beliefs, which cause them to have a misperception or to exaggerate their feelings.

Belief-based Anger

Belief-based anger is anger that is based upon misunderstandings, exaggerations, misinterpretations, wrong beliefs, or lack of faith. Many times children hold anger toward their parents for things that happened in their childhood when they felt their parents had failed them. A child may believe his parents favored one of his siblings and never felt loved as much as that sibling, and this may not be true. It may be that the sibling had a handicap that required the parents to spend more time with him even when the parents loved both children equally. Or a child may feel he was neglected by his parents who were gone much of the time and left him at home alone or required him to play alone for long periods of time. The devil is an opportunist who will take advantage of all such circumstances to plant a lie in the mind of that child and lead them to believe, "If your parents loved you they would not leave you alone like this." This would be an example of belief-based anger. The truth may be that the parent had to work to provide for the child and had no choice in the matter. It was not a matter of choice but of necessity.

One boy I counseled was full of anger at his mother for calling the police on him when he repeatedly brought marijuana into her house. He justified his behavior and stated that he would be happy if she would just let him do what he wanted to do, but he was angry that she refused to let him do this, and he was eventually placed in state custody because of his persistent drug usage. When his mother visited him he was so angry that he refused to see her, and then he ran away from the group home to avoid her completely. His anger was not justified but was lie-based anger.

When anger is belief-based it could be described as "secondary anger" because it is not based upon genuine wrongs but upon misperceptions and misinterpretations of events. The feelings of anger cover up other feelings such as hurt or powerlessness, and it is these other feelings that need to be identified so that the beliefs connected to them can be exposed and replaced with truth. This secondary type of anger or belief-based anger needs to be dealt with by identifying the primary emotion, and all of these other emotions are discussed in section B of this book.

A good example of belief-based or secondary anger is when someone becomes angry at God, which happens quite often. A child whose parent dies is likely to feel anger toward God in addition to strong feelings of grief. If the feelings of grief are first addressed, as is recommend, then there may remain some anger at God for taking the parent away from them during their childhood. Although such feelings of anger toward God are not legitimate or justified anger, they are very real and need to be addressed. It is clear from the Scriptures that God allows painful and evil things to happen to us, but He is not the source of the evil. He is always loving and good. He allowed His own son to be cruelly tortured and crucified, so we know that He allows bad things to happen for a good purpose. Anger toward God or others for such events must be dealt with as belief-based feelings, and all such feelings are discussed in the next section of this book.

Regardless of the type of anger, James 1:19-20 tells us, "Be...slow to anger; for the anger of man does not achieve the righteousness of God." Even when our anger is legitimate we are likely to act out in an unrighteous manner if we hold onto our anger for a long time. And this is why Paul gives us some very useful advice in Ephesians 4:26-27, "Be angry, and yet do not sin; do not let the sun go down on your anger, and do not give the devil an opportunity." Notice that Paul does not say here that we should never be angry, he simply says we should not hold onto it for long.

"Do not let the sun go down on your anger," means to let go of it quickly. In most cases we should let go of our anger by the end of the day. Certainly many husbands and wives are guilty of holding onto their anger too long and would be wise to pay heed to this exhortation and learn to forgive their partners on a daily basis. Most of the offenses that occur between married couples are minor offenses that should be dismissed at the end of the day, and those who remain angry are dooming their marriage to failure. The same is true in relationships with others within a church fellowship. When offenses occur, they should not be allowed to fester and grow into long-term quarrels and anger. Paul concludes this chapter in Ephesians 4: 31-32 with the words, "Let all bitterness and wrath and anger and clamor and slander be put away from you, along with all malice. And be kind to one another, tender-hearted, forgiving each other, just as God in Christ also has forgiven you." Prolonged anger leads to sin.

Sinful Consequences of Anger

Paul's warning in Ephesians 4 is that anger will lead to sin and give the devil a foothold in our lives if we do not release it quickly. There are many ways that we will be led into sin if we allow anger or bitterness to get a foothold in our lives. The most common sinful reaction is to lash out at others with our words, saying angry, hateful words that wound the spirit of our children, our spouse, or our friends. Minor irritations and frustrations caused by children can trigger off strong, angry words and yelling at the child that is disproportionate to the situation. The admonition, "Don't cry over spilled milk" is appropriate to parents who are so stressed and anxious about their child-rearing responsibilities that they sometimes lash out at the child. In Ephesians 6:4 Paul addresses fathers and says, "And fathers, do not provoke your children to anger." Such provocation is often caused by buried anger that the parents have been carrying since their childhood, and it leads to sin and gives the devil a foothold in your life.

Sometimes anger causes Christians to over-react in other ways. One wife confessed in counseling that she was afraid of her husband because of his anger and intimidation. Although her husband was a Christian, he had so much anger inside that he had "road rage" and would literally run other drivers off the road. That was only the public manifestation of his anger. At home he was an angry tyrant who lashed out at his wife for overspending, even though she was the only one who held a full-time job and all the bills were paid through her income. Everyone overreacts at times, but those who habitually do so are likely to have unresolved anger in their life.

Anger will quickly lead to damaged relationships between parent and child, and husband and wife. One young couple sought counseling after being married only a few months. They stated that they had dated for almost a year and had had a wonderful courtship and got along very well during this time, but one week after they were married the husband began to lose his temper and yell at his wife. This hurt her deeply since she had grown up in a household where her mother yelled at her frequently, and she began to respond back in anger. After several months of marriage they were contemplating divorce as a result of anger that they had brought into their relationship.

Eventually anger can lead to criminal behavior or violence. Many juveniles who have grown up in households full of anger begin to rebel during their teenage years and begin getting into fights, using drugs, and engaging in vandalism or criminal activities. Others keep their anger sufficiently controlled to avoid criminal behavior but become violent toward family members. An older couple sought counseling after an incident in which the husband became physically violent and threatening toward his wife. Both of these individuals were Christians but they both had a problem with anger that was keeping them in conflict with one another.

When I met individually with the husband, "Jack," he admitted he had a problem with anger and said he wanted help. We prayed together and he talked about an incident that had occurred fifteen years earlier. He had had a business partner who had embezzled $250,000, and when he was caught he blamed the entire thing on Jack, who could not prove his innocence in the matter. Jack was thrown in jail for six months, lost his marriage, lost his job, lost his reputation, and was placed on probation for 15 years until he could pay back every dollar his partner had stolen. This event had consumed his life for so long that his anger was spilling over into his new marriage, and was destroying his relationship with his wife. I explained to him that he had a right to be angry because of what his partner had done to him, but that this anger was destroying his marriage. I asked him if he would like to get rid of that anger and he said that he would, so I took him through the following steps.

Five Steps to Releasing Fact-based Anger

Some people are unwilling to give up their anger or may be hesitant to do so. Perhaps you feel that you need this anger to protect yourself, or you feel the person needs to be punished and it is your job to do so. Maybe you believe you will be hurt again if you release your anger. Whatever your reason is, pray about this and ask the Lord what He wants you to know. If you are willing to listen to Him He will speak to your mind and remove the lie that is standing in the way. Once you are ready to let God remove your anger, take yourself through the following four steps.

The first step to freedom from anger is to be honest with God about your anger and acknowledge it to God. I led this man in a prayer to God with words like the following: "Lord, when I think about 'John' it makes me very angry. It makes me angry to think about how he stole $250,000 and then lied and blamed it on me. It makes me angry that I lost my job, my wife, and my reputation because of him. And it makes me angry that he got off completely without any consequence and never apologized to me, but I have had to give every last cent I had for the last 15 years to pay off his debt." He was encouraged to simply be honest with God about his anger and he did so.

The next step is to choose to give your anger to God. I continued to lead Jack in prayer with the following words: "But Lord I'm tired of being angry, I'm tired of carrying these feelings and I don't want to carry them any more. So right now I choose to give You these feelings and I ask You to please take them from me and carry them for me." As Jack repeated these words after me I heard a crack in his voice and tears began to roll down his cheeks, but he continued to pray with sincerity and genuineness. He didn't want to continue to live with this anger; he was asking the Lord to take all his anger from him.

The third step is to ask the Lord if there is any truth that He wants you to know, and then listen quietly for the "still, small voice" of God. I prayed for Jack and said, "Lord, You've heard Jack's prayer that You take his anger from him, and I pray right now and ask that You will indeed take these feelings from him, and carry them for him, and replace them with Your peace. And I also ask, Lord, that You would just bring to him any truth that You want him to know right now." Then I said to Jack, "Just listen quietly now in your heart to the 'still, small voice' of God, and tell me if you have any thoughts that come into your mind." After a few moments he said, "I'm just realizing that I need to let go of the past and look to the future. This is all done and past and cannot be changed, but I can do something about the future."

Where do you think that thought came from? I didn't say that to him, but the Lord put those thoughts in his mind. That's how the "still, small voice" of God works. The Holy Spirit just brings the truth to the person's mind that he needs to know at that moment and the result is peace and calm. The truth sets them free from their anger.

The fourth step is to try to stir up the anger to see if it is completely gone. I told this man to think about his former business partner and what he did to him, and try to stir up his anger again. Jack tried to do this but after a few seconds he said, "I don't feel any more anger; it's all gone. Now I just feel sad for him because I realize he was an atheist and he will probably never come to know the Lord." Where do you think that thought came from? I didn't suggest that to him, but the Lord did; He spoke those truthful thoughts into that man's mind and that truth gave him more peace and freedom. In a matter of a few minutes he had gone from pain to peace, and from anger to compassion for this man.

He was feeling sadness, which is another truth-based emotion. I asked him if he would like to get rid of that sadness and he did, so I led him in another prayer to ask the Lord to take his sadness from him, and the Lord took that from him. When people truly forgive others, they begin to feel compassion for their offender, and I saw this miracle take place before my eyes within a few seconds. This is a supernatural event to experience, and it makes my spine tingle and the hair on my arms stand up. It makes me want to bow before the Wonderful Counselor, to see how easily He can release us from our anger and from any destructive emotion.

The fifth step is to identify the remaining feelings and pray again if you still have negative emotions. After this prayer session, this man had a new softness and tenderness toward his wife. He had other emotions that he needed help with, but he began to deal with his inappropriate behaviors toward his wife and to treat her with more love, and he quit losing his temper so quickly. When he got mad he didn't stay mad as long as he used to, and slowly their marriage began to improve. When his wife said things that formerly would have triggered him off, he was able to remain calm and listen. They began to spend more time together and to rebuild their relationship.

Sometimes, individuals who go through this process still have some anger after going through this process. If that occurs, you can simply identify the reason for the continuing anger and pray about it again, adding the new elements they just disclosed to you. Sometimes, people need help in praying about some lie-based anger and other emotions behind their anger, but most of the time you'll find this is all they need to be set free from this anger.

That's what the Wonderful Counselor desires for each of us. We can't eliminate anger on our own, but He wants us to give it all to Him and let Him carry it for us. The Scriptures say about the Lord Jesus in Isaiah 53:4, "Surely, He hath borne our griefs and carried our sorrows" (KJV). The Lord Jesus also said, "Come to me, all who are weary and heavy-laden, and I will give you rest" (Matthew 11:28). Would you like to have that rest? Would you like to be free of this burden of anger, hatred, and resentments? Then give it all to Jesus, the Wonderful Counselor, and let Him carry it for you. And then you can do what the apostle Paul instructed us to do in Ephesians 4:31-32,

"Let all bitterness and wrath and anger and clamor and slander be put away from you, along with all malice. And be kind to one another, tenderhearted, forgiving each other, just as God in Christ also has forgiven you."

Five basic steps to freedom from fact-based anger.
1. Be honest with God and acknowledge all of your anger.
2. Choose to give all of your anger to God and ask Him to carry it for you.
3. Ask the Lord if there is any truth He wants you to know, and then listen to the "still, small voice" of God.
4. Try to stir up the anger again to see if it is all gone.
5. If there is still some anger, then identify the source and repeat steps 1-4.

Suggested Prayer.
Dear Lord, I confess to You that when I think about _____ _____ it makes me angry. It especially makes me angry when I remember _____. But Lord, I'm tired of being angry and I don't want to carry this anger any more. So right now I choose to give it to You, and I ask You to please take it from me and carry it for me, and replace it with Your peace. And I also ask that You bring to me any truth that You want me to know right now. I pray this in Jesus' name. Amen

CHAPTER 4

Releasing Feelings of Sadness and Disappointment

One of the classic old hymns of the fait, written by Joseph M. Scriven, is "What a Friend We Have in Jesus." As I have learned to take my troubles to the Lord in prayer I have come to appreciate the words of this hymn more and more.

> *What a friend we have in Jesus, All our sins and griefs to bear!*
> *What a privilege to carry Everything to God in prayer!*
> *O what peace we often forfeit, O what needless pain we bear,*
> *All because we do not carry Everything to God in prayer!*

The hymn writer is correct that when we learn to take our emotions to the Lord in prayer and to leave them with Him, He is able to release us from them, whatever they may be. The second verse of this song goes on to say, "Have we trials and temptations? Is there trouble anywhere? We should never be discouraged. Take it to the Lord in prayer." Is that statement true, that "we should never be discouraged"? We can know for certain that we will sometimes experience times of sadness and disappointment in our life, regardless of how spiritually mature we are, but what about discouragement? Is discouragement the same as disappointment or is it different? We'll take a look at these questions at the end of this chapter.

Times of Sadness

According to the 1998 *Oxford American Desk Dictionary* (Oxford Unversity Press, 1998) the word "sad" comes from the old English word "saed" which means "sated" or "weary," and from a Germanic word that means "weighty" or "dense." We sometimes feel an emotional heaviness or weightiness when we learn about unhappy events or come to an unhappy realization or understanding about a life circumstance. Those who are "weary" and weighed down with emotion need to hear the words of the Lord Jesus, who said, "Come to Me, all who are weary and heavy-laden, and I will give you rest" (Matthew 11:28).

There are times when tragedies occur that cause us to feel the emotion of sadness. When a friend or acquaintance has an unpleasant experience you may feel a deep sadness and concern for them. You may hear that a child of theirs has had a serious accident, or they have contracted a serious illness, or given birth to a child with serious handicaps. A close friend of our daughter's dove head first into a shallow creek at a Bible camp and broke his neck when he hit the bottom. This lively, enjoyable child was permanently paralyzed from the neck down as a result of this accident, and those who knew him well were deeply saddened by this unfortunate event.

Sometimes you may see a child who is born without any legs and you may feel a deep sadness for the child and for the parents of that child. You may hear about a young mother with three pre-school children whose husband died and who was left without any visible means of support, and you may feel sadness that these children will never know their father and that the father will never be able to see his children grow into adulthood. These are sad circumstances, and if you know such individuals personally or see such people regularly you may experience deep feelings of sadness. If it is your own child who has experienced a tragic situation you may feel deeply saddened for them for a long time.

At other times, a new realization or insight into a situation may provoke feelings of sadness. One young woman spent a prayer session praying about some childhood abuse she had endured from her father, and she was able to release her feelings of anger toward him that had caused her to overreact emotionally toward all the men in her life. After praying and asking the Lord to take her feelings of anger from her I asked her, "How do you feel now as you think about your father's cruel behavior, whipping you until you had blisters, and forcing you to wear clothes that caused the other children to tease you?" She stated, "I'm no longer angry toward him. He just did what he did out of the brokenness in his own life." I then asked her, "As you think about this memory do you have any other negative feelings?" She replied, "I feel a sadness that we didn't have a closer relationship all of those years and missed out on some wonderful times we could have had if he had not believed so many lies." I agreed with this young lady that it was indeed sad. It is always sad to see how lies and warped thinking prevent individuals from enjoying a happy life or a happy relationship with their parents or children. It is sad when you realize how much joy you missed earlier in your life due to twisted thinking and distorted beliefs of your own or of others.

Sadness of the Lord

Twice when the Lord Jesus and His disciples approached Jerusalem He wept over the city. On the first occasion, recorded for us in Luke 13:34-35, we're told that He cried out "O Jerusalem, Jerusalem, the city that kills the prophets and stones those sent to her! How often I wanted to gather your children together, just as a hen gathers her brood under her wings, and you would not have it! Behold, your house is left to you desolate; and I say to you, you shall not see Me until the time comes when you say, 'Blessed is He who comes in the name of the Lord!'" Although we are not told specifically that He wept, it is clear from the language that He used that He was filled with strong emotions as He spoke these sad words to the city and the people that He loved.

The second occasion occurred the week before His crucifixion, as He made his "triumphal entry" into the city and the crowds were praising God joyfully and casting their garments on the ground before Him. It is recorded for us in Luke 19:41 that "when He approached, He saw the city and wept over it." The reason for His sadness is found in His words in the following three verses, where Jesus expressed His sadness at knowing that they were going to reject Him, and that as a result that beautiful city was going to be completely destroyed in a few years "because you did not recognize the time of your visitation" (Luke 19:44).

This was an anticipatory sadness, not at something that had already happened but at something that He knew was going to happen in a short while. It is like the "anticipatory grief" that people sometimes experience when they know that someone they love has a fatal disease and that their condition is progressively worsening and will continue to worsen until they die. Such circumstances can lead to a deep sadness like that experienced by the Lord Jesus on these two occasions while He was approaching the city of Jerusalem.

The reaction of the Lord Jesus is helpful, because it shows us that sadness is sometimes normal and based upon truth and reality rather than wrong beliefs or lack of faith. The Lord was full of truth, and yet He was sad on a number of occasions. Sadness is sometimes intensified by lies and wrong beliefs, though it is usually based upon facts and the truth. But the Lord does not want us to live in such a state. He wants us to give Him these feelings, and He wants to relieve us of them so that they do not hinder our spiritual walk or diminish our joy, even while we face sad circumstances. The Lord Jesus experienced sadness, disappointment and grief, but He did not remain entrenched in these feelings for a long time. He knew how to release them quickly, and He wants us to release them as well so that they do not hinder our fruitfulness.

The Sadness of Nehemiah

In Nehemiah 1:1-3 we read that when one of Nehemiah's brothers and some other men from Judah came to him in Susa, the capital city of Persia, in the month of Chisley, he inquired about the Jews who had survived the captivity and about the city of Jerusalem. They said to Nehemiah, "The remnant there in the province who survived the captivity are in great distress and reproach, and the wall of Jerusalem is broken down and its gates are burned with fire." Nehemiah wrote, "Now it came about when I heard these words, I sat down and wept and mourned for days; and I was fasting and praying before the God of heaven"(v. 4).

His sadness continued for at least a month because we're told in Nehemiah 2:1-3 that it was in the month of Nisan when he was serving the king as his cupbearer that the king noticed that he was sad. Nehemiah stated that he had never been sad in the king's presence before and it frightened him when the king asked him why he was sad. The king asked him, "Why is your face sad though you are not sick? This is nothing but sadness of heart" (Nehemiah 2:2). Nehemiah was still deeply saddened about the news of the destruction of Jerusalem and how it lay in ruins. He remembered the glory of the city when it was vibrant and strong and now, as he pictured it lying in ruins, he could not shake his sadness.

Imagine how it would feel if you had spent time in Washington, D.C., enjoying all of the national landmarks and visiting the White House and touring the capitol building, and then were carried away into captivity by an invading army. Years later someone who has just returned from Washington, D.C., tells you that they just came from there and the entire city has been destroyed and burned to the ground. The White House and the Capitol building had been burned and razed to the ground, the Washington monument and the Lincoln Memorial were completely destroyed and there was nothing but ashes and shattered stones remaining in the Capitol city. You would probably feel great sadness at such news, and returning to see the destruction would sadden you even more.

This is what made Nehemiah sad. His sadness was understandable and justifiable, not a result of emotional weakness. It is okay and normal to feel deep sadness at times, and it may be difficult to overcome such feelings. Like Nehemiah, you may have such feelings for months, and sometimes there is nothing you can do about the cause of your sadness. You may feel that you can never be as happy again as you once were, and you may feel overwhelmed with your sadness. Although such feelings are normal, and you may be unable to overcome your sadness on your own, the Lord is able to take those feelings from you and restore you to full joy and peace once again. You don't have to live with those feelings of sadness for the rest of your life.

Times of Disappointment

Disappointment has a more specific meaning than sadness and refers to shattered expectations or failure to fulfill a desire or expectation. Some disappointments are mild and some are very deep. For example, you may attend a football game about which you are excited and become disappointed when your team loses. This would probably be a very mild disappointment unless your child was playing on the losing team and he was very distraught at his performance. Your disappointment may be more intense in such circumstances where the disappointment personally affects you in some way.

When our son was a teenager he often competed in music competitions, and my wife and I attended all of his performances and tried to encourage him regardless of how well he performed. There were times that he performed well and won the competitions and there were times when he practiced for long, long hours and performed well but lost the competition. We sometime felt a sadness for him and a disappointment that he lost competitions for which he had practiced so diligently and worked so hard to prepare. This is a natural sadness and disappointment.

Disappointment is sometimes magnified by distorted beliefs and unrealistic expectations that people have, but it is a natural experience at other times. Sometimes people you know intimately and love dearly disappoint you seriously, and your feelings of disappointment are very intense. There are many examples of pastors in our country who have been very influential and blessed hundreds or thousands of Christians through their ministry, and then fell into sexual temptations or were publicly shamed due to some illegal behaviors. Those who loved and supported them, even after the accusations were made, are sometimes deeply disappointed when the truth comes out and the accused person finally admits the truth. Such feelings of betrayal and disappointment are very strong and are based upon the truth, not based upon naiveté or distorted beliefs.

A friend of mine was devastated when his wife suddenly declared that she was in love with another man and she was leaving him. He felt many powerful feelings including abandonment, failure, rejection, and anger, and made repeated attempts to persuade his wife not to leave him and to go with him for counseling for the sake of their child. While still seeking to be reconciled with her, he learned that his best friend and his wife had invited the man's wife and her new boyfriend for a meal at their house, not in order to persuade them to separate so she could return to her husband, but to show friendship to them. My friend was rightfully angry and disappointed in his friend. This did not destroy their friendship, but serious disappointment will often affect a relationship in significant ways.

The Disappointment of the Lord

After the resurrection of the Lord Jesus He was astounded at the lack of belief of His disciples and He rebuked them (Mark 16:10-14). This appears to be an example of the Lord Jesus being disappointed in the disciples. It's very interesting that the Lord Jesus would feel such strong emotion that He would rebuke them after the resurrection for their unbelief, because He knew what was in the heart of all men, and we're told in Psalm 103:13-14 that "Just as a father has compassion on his children, so the Lord has compassion on those who fear Him. For He Himself knows our frame; He is mindful that we are but dust." In this instance the Lord Jesus was nonetheless disappointed that they were so slow to believe in His resurrection, even though He had clearly told them about it previously. While talking to the two men on the Emmaus road who were saddened and grief-stricken over the death of the Lord, Jesus said to them "O foolish men and slow of heart to believe in all that the prophets have spoken!" (Luke 24: 25).

Even the enemies of the Lord remembered that He had prophesied His own resurrection and had publicly stated that He would rise again on the third day, and this led them to request a squad of Roman guards to guard the tomb and to seal it (Matthew 27:62-66). But the disciples of Jesus were slow to believe, and the Lord Jesus was amazed at their lack of belief and lack of understanding. In Mark 16:14 it states that, "He reproached them for their unbelief and hardness of heart, because they had not believed those who had seen Him after He had risen." Abraham obeyed God and was willing to sacrifice his only son Isaac because "He considered that God is able to raise men even from the dead; from which he also received him back as a type," according to Hebrews 11:19. But after spending three years with His disciples and performing miracle after miracle, even raising the dead, they still did not understand or believe that Jesus could raise Himself from the dead. When many of His followers began reporting sightings of the Lord on the third day, there were still many who refused to believe them, and this was disappointing to the Lord.

The fact that the Lord Jesus experienced feelings of disappointment proves that feelings of disappointment are sometimes fact-based feelings that are natural and are not the result of wrong thinking or wrong beliefs. The Lord Jesus had no wrong beliefs or distorted thinking, since He was God, but He was sometimes disappointed in His disciples. The same is true for each of us. Sometimes friends and family members do things that are very disappointing and it is normal and natural to be upset and disappointed in them, and the Lord is able to give us His peace when we find ourselves feeling disappointed in others for good, legitimate reasons.

The Disappointment of David

The Psalmist David experienced feelings of disappointment also. All of us have been disappointed in others at times, whether it is with our family members or with other Christians we have trusted with our personal feelings. Most of us have had enemies who disliked or hated us for unknown and unjustified reasons, and that is a troubling and confusing experience. But David experienced an enormous amount of opposition and hostility due to his position as King of Israel, in spite of how loved he was by many of the citizens of the country. The same level of hostility can be found against any good leader, no matter how sincere, hard-working, godly or compassionate, and David felt a ton of hostility from his many enemies.

In Psalm 69: 3-4 he wrote, "I am weary with my crying; my throat is parched; My eyes fail while I wait for my God. Those who hate me without a cause are more than the hairs of my head; those who would destroy me are powerful." Notice how overwhelmed he is, and saddened at the opposition he feels from his enemies. He wept until his throat was parched and his eyes could not see, and he cried out for the Lord to deliver him.

In Psalm 41:9 he speaks of another disappointment; the disappointment of discovering that even his friends betrayed him. He wrote, "Even my close friend in whom I trusted, Who ate my bread, Has lifted up his heel against me." David had many enemies and individuals who hated him without cause, but what amazed and disappointed him even more was when some of his closest and most trusted friends turned out to be working against him and conspiring with his enemies against him. Imagine what that would be like, to have a close friend who eats at your house for years, who turns against you and betrays you like an enemy.

This painful feeling of disappointment is brought out even more poignantly in Psalm 55:12-14. David complained in this psalm of how his heart was in anguish and he was overwhelmed with fear and trembling because of the hostility of his enemies, but the worst part of his anguish was due to some of his closest friends turning against him. He wrote, "For it is not an enemy who reproaches me, Then I could bear it; Nor is it one who hates me who has exalted himself against me, Then I could hide myself from him. But it is you, a man my equal, My companion and my familiar friend. We who had sweet fellowship together, Walked in the house of God in the throng." He was in such deep anguish because of the disappointment brought about by his closest friends. It is such a painful feeling to be disappointed by close friends and family members

Perhaps this has happened in your life. You have been seriously betrayed and disappointed by a close friend. Maybe it was your spouse who forsook his or her marriage vows and left you for another person. At one time you were deeply in love with your spouse and shared your innermost feelings and thoughts, and then you became estranged and the one who had been your closest friend became your worst enemy and sought to harm you in any conceivable way. Such circumstances create feelings of genuine disappointment, in addition to other feelings, all of which need to be released so that you can become a productive, fruitful person once again. Such disappointments are usually truth-based and fact-based feelings, but the Lord desires to release you from such negative feelings so that they will not hold you in bondage.

Discouragement vs. Disappointment

Before discussing how we can overcome feelings of sadness and disappointment, I want to first make a few comments about feelings of discouragement. The song referred to at the beginning of this chapter says, "We should never be discouraged. Take it to the Lord in prayer." What exactly is discouragement, and is it the same as disappointment?

The definition of disappointment used earlier refers to shattered expectations or feelings of sadness due to the failure to fulfill a desire or expectation. Sometimes people deeply disappoint us by their behavior or their words. Discouragement, on the other hand, means, literally, to lose courage. According to the *Oxford American Desk Dictionary* (1998 edition), "discourage" means to "deprive of courage, confidence, or energy."

You may become discouraged by circumstances, such as when you try to save money only to find that two of your cars break down and, not only are all your savings consumed, but you become more deeply indebted. Under these circumstances you may feel like giving up and not trying to save money or stay out of debt. That is one type of discouragement, and it is a mild feeling of hopelessness. You may become discouraged at your efforts to achieve a personal goal and feel hopeless about achieving it. For example, you may have aspirations to be a professional athlete, and yet the competition is so strong that you eventually become discouraged and give up your goal. Your feelings of discouragement in such a case may be well founded and the Lord may use these circumstances to redirect your life goals. Such feelings of discouragement and hopelessness may be so intense because you believe the lie that you are a worthless person unless you achieve that goal. The Lord may use these circumstances to expose your false beliefs and to redirect your life in some major way. When feelings of discouragement lead to hopelessness about life, such feelings are always belief-based and not fact-based, and need to be submitted to the Lord to be challenged and replaced with His truth.

Sometimes we may become discouraged about matters that we know are within God's will because the Scriptures make it clear that the Lord wants us to accomplish them. For example, we may become discouraged about losing weight to keep our bodies healthy, trying to live a Christian life, or trying to overcome a specific sin or weakness. The Scriptures tell us clearly that the Lord desires us to live holy lives, and He has given believers a new nature and His Holy Spirit to empower them to overcome the sin. So we know that we should not give in to discouragement and just give up. When we know it is God's will for us to achieve something, we should never be discouraged but, as the hymn writer says, "take it to the Lord in prayer."

A biblical example of how we should deal with discouragement is found, once again, in the life of Nehemiah. As Nehemiah began the work of rebuilding the walls around Jerusalem, many of the inhabitants of the land did everything in their power to discourage them, including ridiculing them and threatening to kill them. In Nehemiah 6:9 we are told explicitly, "For all of them were trying to frighten us, thinking, 'They will become discouraged with the work and it will not be done.' But now, O God, strengthen my hands." Nehemiah called the workers together and encouraged them. When he saw their fear he said to the workers, "Do not be afraid of them; remember the Lord who is great and awesome, and fight for your brothers, your sons, your daughters, your wives, and your houses"(Nehemiah 4:14). He then organized the workers and set up a guard and they continued to rebuild the wall until it was finally completed.

Discouragement in this case was based upon fear, which was based upon lies and distorted beliefs. When this is the case we need to do as Nehemiah did and challenge those fears with the truth. Fears are always belief-based, and more specific steps for overcoming fears will be discussed in Chapter 7. Disappointment is fact-based, whereas discouragement is belief-based, so the song writer is correct in saying that "we should never be discouraged. Take it to the Lord in prayer." However, we will sometimes become disappointed even when we know the truth and are living according to the truth. Let's look now at how to overcome feelings of sadness or disappointment through prayer.

Overcoming Sadness and Disappointment

Sadness and Disappointment are fact-based emotions just like justified anger and grief, and the way to overcome them is the same as the way for overcoming grief and anger: by giving them to the Lord. Some key verses are given, below. Notice what each of these Scriptures says or implies about how we can deal with our grief, our sorrow, our cares, and our emotional burdens. "Surely our griefs He Himself bore, And our sorrows He carried" (Isaiah 53:4). "Casting all your care upon Him, for He careth for you" (1 Peter 5:7, KJV). "Come to Me, all who are weary and heavy-laden, and I will give you rest" (Matthew 11:28). "Cast your burden upon the Lord, and He will sustain you; He will never allow the righteous to be shaken" (Psalm 55:22).

There is a hymn that says to "Take your burdens to the Lord and leave them there." This is sometimes a cliché used by Christians to encourage fellow believers and it is usually unhelpful, although there is a great deal of truth behind those words. However, we must understand which emotions can be dealt with in this fashion. The basic prayer principle involved in finding release from fact-based emotions is the principle of learning to cast your burdens upon the Lord.

The young lady mentioned earlier who still felt sadness after forgiving her father for his abusive behavior went through this same procedure to release both her anger and then her sadness. I asked her if she would like to get rid of this sadness and she stated that she would. I then led her in a prayer that went something like this: "Lord, when I think about my father and how he used to treat me, it makes me sad that he was so confused and thought he was doing the right thing. And it makes me sad to realize how much better our relationship could have been if he had not been so strict and so harsh with me. I wish that we had been much closer. But Lord, I'm tired of feeling this sadness and I don't want to carry it any more, so I choose right now to give it to You and I ask You to please carry it for me. I give it to You now, in Jesus' name. Amen."

After she gave these feelings to the Lord I prayed briefly for her and asked the Lord to take those feelings of sadness from her, and then I prayed and asked the Lord to bring to her any truth that He wanted her to know (the second major prayer principle). She stated that she had no new thoughts other than knowing that her father did the best he knew at the time, and that she could still look forward to enjoying him more in the future, and still have a close relationship with him.

There are five simple steps to releasing your feelings of sadness and disappointment. First, be honest with the Lord and acknowledge the full extent of your sadness and disappointment and why you feel it. Second, ask the Lord to take those feelings from you and carry them for you as He promised He would. Third, ask the Lord what He wants you to know, and then listen quietly to the "still, small voice of God." Be sure that your thoughts are consistent with the Word of God, and pray with a friend if necessary, who is knowledgeable of the Scriptures. Fourth, after receiving some healing, think about your sadness and disappointment and try to stir up the pain again to see if it is still present. Fifth, if there is still some remaining pain in the memory, identify what is painful about it and pray again.

If other painful feelings surface, identify them and pray with someone who knows how to pray about belief-based pain (this will be covered in Chapters 5-12) to see all of them removed.

You may say the following prayer, if you find it useful. As you pray this prayer, fill in the blanks with the appropriate name and information. Then afterwards meditate quietly and see what thoughts the Lord might bring to your mind to give you His perfect peace. Once He gives you His peace, take the time to thank Him for what He just did for you.

Dear Lord, as I think about _____ it makes me sad (or disappointed) because _____. But Lord, I'm tired of feeling this sadness (or disappointment) and pain, so right now I choose to give it to You, and I ask You to please take it from me, and carry it for me, and replace it with Your peace. I also ask that You bring to me any truth that You want me to know right now. I pray this in Jesus' name. Amen

CHAPTER 5

Dealing with Truth-based Guilt

In the first chapter we discussed the emotions of the Lord Jesus and observed that He experienced a wide range of human emotions during his earthly walk. The emotions he felt were all fact-based feelings because He had no false beliefs that gave rise to feelings of fear, rejection, shame, helplessness, or hopelessness; nonetheless, He sometimes became deeply troubled and disturbed. All of His negative feelings were fact-based feelings of sadness, grief, disappointment, and righteous anger. He even experienced aloneness as a fact-based emotion, although for us it is a belief-based emotion since we are never truly alone with God in our lives. There is one fact-based emotion that we all experience, however, that the Lord Jesus never experienced, and that is genuine guilt.

Genuine Guilt

We all fall short of God's standards and experience genuine guilt at times. This needs to be clearly distinguished from false guilt and shame which many people experience, and which will be dealt with in another chapter. Romans 3:23 says "all have sinned and fall short of the glory of God." This means that every person experiences genuine guilt at times, because every person fails and violates God's standards at times. The person who denies this is described in the Scriptures as "deceiving himself" (1 John 1:8) and a liar. But the Lord Jesus never fell short and never sinned, so He never experienced the emotion of guilt. And because we all fall short and sin, we must know how to deal effectively with true feelings of guilt, because if we fail to do so we will suppress them until they begin to affect our behavior in many ways.

King David was described in the Scriptures as "a man after His [God's] own heart" (1 Samuel 13:14) and yet he sinned grievously on several occasions. He wrote about his painful feelings of guilt in Psalm 32: 3-5.

> "When I kept silent about my sin, my body wasted away Through my groaning all day long. For day and night Thy hand was heavy upon me; My vitality was drained away as with the fever-heat of summer. I acknowledged my sin to Thee, And my iniquity I did not hide; I said, 'I will confess my transgressions to the Lord'; And Thou didst forgive the guilt of my sin."

In this passage David states that his "body wasted away" and his "vitality was drained away." This means that he experienced physical problems as a result of his unresolved guilt feelings and he lacked energy as a result of his sin. When he finally confessed his sins, he was forgiven, however, and his soul was restored again, as he wrote in Psalms 23:3, "He restoreth my soul" (KJV).

When we fail to deal promptly with our sins and our failures we subject ourselves to similar consequences. We are likely to experience emotional pain and stress, spiritual separation from God, social alienation from others whom we have wronged, and eventually physical symptoms. Our literature is full of stories based upon such themes, such as in Shakespeare's *Macbeth* when Lady Macbeth plotted with her husband to kill the King and then tried in vain to wash off the blood stains from her hands. In Nathaniel Hawthorne's *The Scarlet Letter,* a Puritan pastor began to wither away physically, lost weight, and became sickly, eventually dying, due to his hidden sin of adultery. Edgar Allen Poe wrote the short story called *The Tell-Tale Heart* which described how the soul of a man was tormented day and night by his knowledge of having murdered a man and buried his body under the floorboards of his house. When the police come to investigate complaints from the neighbors, the murderer imagines he hears the murdered man's heart beating louder and louder, until in a frenzy he confesses his crime to the police.

Although these examples are fictional they attest to the common consequences of sin that we all experience at times, in some degree or other when we fail. When we do fall short of God's standards we have three choices of how to deal with it. First, we can *suppress* it and pretend it wasn't a failure at all. However, no matter how long we suppress it, it can continue to affect us until we are able to completely eliminate it. Although this is probably the most common method of dealing with guilt, it is not effective and it has long-term psychological consequences. Second, we can *express* it by talking with others about it, with a therapist or friend or by writing about it in some disguised form and attempting to release it. Third, we can *confess* it to God and seek to release it through spiritual means. This will be discussed in much greater detail in a subsequent section of this chapter.

The Psychological Consequences of Guilt

The *AA*[Alcoholics Anonymous] *Big Book* speaks of the importance of dealing with guilt. In the twelve steps to sobriety that are outlined in that book, seven of the steps are devoted to the process of cleansing the conscience of the alcoholic. Step two says "We made a searching and fearless moral inventory of ourselves" and step ten says "We continued to take personal inventory, and when we were wrong promptly admitted it." All of the intermediate steps provide more details about the process that AA recommends for their members to take to clear their consciences. This gives strong testimony to the powerfully destructive and controlling influence that guilt can have upon an individual, which must be removed before they can be free of their addictions.

Guilt can affect us in many ways emotionally and psychologically. Some people have such strong self-loathing and guilt that they become self abusive and cut on themselves. In some countries and cultures, people flagellate themselves with whips until they bleed, or they crawl on their knees for miles to show their repentance. Some individuals in other parts of the world submit themselves to actual crucifixions in order to show their penitence.

In our culture there has been a recent revision of various forms of bodily mutilations which they call "body art" and "body piercings." Some individuals take pleasure in the number of piercings they can get, with piercings in their skull, their eyelids, their ears, their tongue, their nipples, their navel, and every other conceivable body part. Although this may be motivated by a desire for attention or defiance of societal standards, it is often related to feelings of self-loathing and a desire to punish themselves for things they have done.

Some individuals known as "masochists" appear to take pleasure in their own physical pain, which sounds like a contradiction of terms. However, the reason for their apparently irrational behavior is the deep-seated feelings of self-hatred and guilt that they feel. Some of these feelings are genuine guilt and some are false guilt or shame, which will be discussed in a later chapter.

Albert Ellis, a renowned psychologist who is the founder of a form of cognitive therapy called "Rational-Emotive Psychotherapy", describes the case of a young woman who was a masochist and went to a therapist to receive help for her condition. In his book, *A New Guide to Rational Living (1975)*, he described how she often engaged in painful acts of sexual degradation and self-injury, and her therapist explored some of the historical factors behind her masochistic behaviors. It turned out that she experienced strong feelings of guilt and self-loathing from having been sexually abused as a child, and she continued to engage in such punishing acts against herself to deal with her feelings of guilt. Her therapist focused upon helping her challenge some of her deeply-rooted feelings of guilt in order to free her from this destructive behavior pattern.

Secular Solutions

This example illustrates one of the major rifts that is often found between professional therapists and Christian counselors or pastors when trying to help people who are in emotional distress. Several studies have confirmed that there is a strong atheistic bias among professional psychologists, and that their values are widely discrepant from those of their clients, 90% of whom profess to have strong spiritual beliefs while only 20% of the psychologists profess to have similar beliefs. Dr. Ellis openly states that he believes religions foster neuroticism and irrational thinking that is psychologically destructive to individuals.

In many of Dr. Ellis's writings he advocates that individuals who have moral issues and guilt should engage in outrageous behaviors, to enable them to do what they want without regard for the opinions and judgments of others. His solution for guilt is to rationalize it, minimize it, challenge the validity of any guilt feelings, and engage in guilt-producing behaviors until the person no longer feels any pangs of guilt.

There are many workshops available for mental health professionals, but over my 30 year time span in the mental health profession I have never seen one that deals specifically with guilt. The concept of guilt is generally treated as an unhealthy, neurotic product of religion. There is one notable exception, however, among those mental health professionals who deal with sexual offenders. They recognize the value of genuine guilt, and many of them believe that the most dangerous sexual offenders are those who are psychopathic and lack a normal conscience. Many of the most prominent researchers in this specialized field recommend that sex offenders need to hold onto their guilt, because they believe it will help prevent them from engaging in future harmful actions.

The Biblical Solution

In contrast to the attempts of secular psychologists to help clients rationalize their sin or minimize it, which only results in the suppression of their emotions, the Scriptures instruct us in how to be released from the guilt of our sins through forgiveness.

All throughout the Old Testament it was proclaimed that God is a compassionate and forgiving God who would forgive those who repented and confessed their sins to God. There are many Scriptures that can be used as the basis for this but the following are some of my favorite ones.

> But Thou art a God of forgiveness, Gracious and compassionate, Slow to anger and abounding in lovingkindness; And Thou didst not forsake them. Nehemiah 9:17

> To the Lord our God belong compassion and forgiveness... Daniel 9:9

> I acknowledged my sin to Thee, And my iniquity I did not hide; I said, "I will confess my transgressions to the Lord." Psalm 32:5

> For as high as the heavens are above the earth, So great is His lovingkindness toward those who fear Him. As far as the east is from the west, So far has He removed our transgressions from us. Psalm 103:11-12

> Who is a God like Thee, who pardons iniquity And passes over the rebellious act of the remnant of His possession? He does not retain His anger forever, Because He delights in unchanging love. He will again have compassion on us; He will tread our iniquities underfoot. Yes, Thou wilt cast all their sins into the depths of the sea. Micah 7:18-19

Although the Old Testament Scriptures proclaimed the compassion and forgiveness of God, it was not until Jesus came as the Messiah and died for our sins that the basis for our forgiveness was proclaimed, namely, the substitutionary sacrifice of Jesus as the "Lamb of God." The New Testament Scriptures teach that those who repent of their sins and receive Jesus as their Savior will be forgiven and have eternal life. See the following New Testament Scriptures for a few references.

The Son of Man has authority on earth to forgive sins. Luke 5:24

Of Him all the prophets bear witness that through His name every one who believes in Him receives forgiveness of sins. Acts 10:43

And when you were dead in your transgressions and the uncircumcision of your flesh, He made you alive together with Him, having forgiven us all our transgressions. Colossians 2:13

All things are cleansed with blood, and without shedding of blood there is no forgiveness. Hebrews 9:22

Behold, the Lamb of God who takes away the sin of the world! John 1:29

If we confess our sins, He is faithful and righteous to forgive us our sins and to cleanse us from all unrighteousness. 1 John 1:9

Thus, the Christian solution for guilt is to admit it, to repent of our sins, and confess them to the Lord. Attempts to minimize, rationalize, or suppress our guilt will only result in unresolved feelings of genuine guilt that can only be removed through the forgiveness that comes through Christ. Those who carry a burden of guilt and suffer the emotional and spiritual consequences of sin are like the character named "Christian" in *Pilgrim's Progress,* who began reading the Bible and woke up one morning to discover that he had a huge burden strapped to his back that he could not remove. When he ran to the cross the burden simply slid off his back and was left behind. What a wonderful thing it is to have your sins and guilt removed, as David stated in Psalm 32:1, "How blessed is he whose transgression is forgiven, Whose sin is covered!"

Confronting Clients with Sin

Some Christians do not recognize their sin. They recognize other negative emotions but are so full of anger, hurt, and feelings of hopelessness that they cannot feel their guilt until the other emotions are first removed. Such was the case of "Sandy", a Christian woman who came for counseling because of some feelings of hurt and anger toward her husband. She mentioned incidentally that she had been married previously and had left her first husband when she had an affair with her second husband. After she had resolved her feelings of hurt and anger toward her present husband I asked her, "How does it feel now when you think about how your husband has hurt you and wronged you?"

"I just feel neutral and calm about it now. I realize that it was due to his issues and not mine; it wasn't my fault."

"So, think about your feelings now. Does that clear up your negative feelings or are there any other negative feelings you have, now that you have resolved these feelings toward 'Joe'?" I asked her.

Sandy paused for a minute to reflect on her feelings. After a brief period of contemplation she replied, "I guess that I feel some guilt about the affair I had with Joe when we first met. I never thought much about it before, but now I feel badly that I had that affair with him. I think I probably should deal with that."

I never had to confront Sandy with this sin. Yes, when she first mentioned her affair with Joe I made a mental note of it and realized that it was one of the issues that she needed to deal with eventually. But I focused on the most prominent negative emotion that she wanted help with, knowing that eventually the guilt would probably surface and we could deal with that.

It's interesting to notice that Jesus dealt with the Samaritan woman in John 4 in a similar fashion. Jesus knew from the beginning of His conversation with her that she was a sinful woman. He knew that she was living with a man now who was not her husband, and that she had been married five times previously, but He did not immediately confront her with this.

He spoke with her kindly and ministered to her emotional and spiritual needs, and when He did mention that she had no husband, He did not apparently say it in a condemning way. Jesus was simply letting her know that He knew all about her, and He spoke with her about living water that would satisfy her thirst (emotional longings and needs) permanently.

We find the same pattern in John 8 when He dealt with the woman caught in adultery. The religious leaders dragged her into the Temple where Jesus was teaching and asked Him whether they should stone her as the law of Moses demanded, or release her. Their motives were corrupt; they were not concerned about what to do with her. They simply were looking for an opportunity to accuse Him of something, and Jesus, knowing their hearts, knelt down and wrote something on the ground. When they persisted in asking Him what they should do with the woman Jesus finally stood up and said to them, "He who is without sin among you, let him be the first to throw a stone at her" (John 8:7). The crowd began to disperse, beginning with the oldest and down to the youngest until only Jesus and the woman were left there. Jesus asked her, "Woman, where are they? Did no one condemn you?" And she said, "No one, Lord." And Jesus said, "Neither do I condemn you; go your way; from now on sin no more" (John 8:10-11).

Notice that Jesus did not confront her with her sin and tell her that she needed to confess her sin. No, He knew she was aware of her sin and she had already repented of it, because of her attitude and because she called him "Lord." He simply spoke the truth to her that He did not condemn her either; she was already forgiven because she had already repented of her sin.

The Freedom of Forgiveness

So, how exactly can you find freedom from genuine guilt? Suppose, for example, that you have committed a serious sin and you want to be forgiven and to be at peace again? What are the steps that you can take to release your guilt?

1 John 1:9 tells us that, "If we confess our sins, He is faithful and righteous to forgive us our sins and to cleanse us

from all unrighteousness." First, admit to God your guilt and moral failure. Second, confess your sins to God, asking for His forgiveness through the blood of Jesus. Third, thank the Lord for the promises in His Word that He forgives and cleanses us from all our sins, and thank Him for forgiving you today.

After going through these three steps you are promised in this Scripture that you have been forgiven and you can claim this promise. Some people, however, do not feel forgiven even though they are, because they have internal lies that are creating false guilt which will keep them in bondage to these emotions. If this is the case for you, find a mature prayer partner who can take you through the process described in Chapter 11 for dealing with shame and false guilt.

You may also find it helpful to say the following prayer. As you pray this prayer, fill in the blanks with the appropriate information. Then afterwards meditate quietly and see what thoughts the Lord might bring to your mind to give you His perfect peace. Once He gives you His peace, take the time to thank Him for what He just did for you.

Dear Lord, as I think about my sin, especially about _____ _____, I know that I am guilty and I have broken your laws. But Lord, I'm tired of carrying this guilt and pain, so right now I confess my sins to You and ask You to forgive me, through the blood of Jesus, who died for me. I ask You, Lord, to please take my sins from me, and cast them in the deepest sea. I also ask that You bring to me any truth that You want me to know right now. I pray this In Jesus' name. Amen

SECTION B

DEALING WITH BELIEF-BASED EMOTIONS

Prayer Principle 2: James 1:5

"If any of you lacks wisdom, let him ask of God."

CHAPTER 6

Principles for Dealing with Belief-based Emotions

Storms are often used by the Lord to teach us important lessons, and to expose our true character and beliefs. When I was a child I lived in Kansas, which is sometimes referred to as the "tornado capital of the world." Every summer as a child I was confronted with tornados that threatened our family and our home, and I quickly developed a fear of storms. Since we lived in a ranch style home with no basement we were vulnerable to tornados, and when the tornado sirens sounded my mother would take me and my four siblings in our car and drive around the neighborhood looking up at the sky to see if we could spot any funnel clouds. We planned to dash into one of the nearby houses under construction in our neighborhood that had a basement if we ever sighted a tornado funnel, although this never happened. However, the Lord used these storms to confront me with my vulnerability and mortality, and this eventually led me to turn to the Lord for my salvation. God also used these storms in my life to expose my fears, and He removed my fears of storms after I became a believer.

In the Scriptures, storms are often used as a metaphor of our life struggles. The Lord Jesus used this metaphor at the end of the Sermon on the Mount when He said, "every one who hears these words of Mine, and acts upon them, may be compared to a wise man who built his house upon the rock. And the rain descended, and the floods came, and the winds blew, and burst against that house; and yet it did not fall, for it had been founded on the rock" (Matthew 7:24-25). I want to talk about storms in this chapter and how the Lord uses storms to expose our false beliefs and to give us peace.

Mark 4:35-41 records for us an experience with storms in the life of the Lord's disciples that illustrates four important principles for helping us find peace in the midst of storms. Jesus had been teaching his disciples and a multitude of curious people all day long, periodically taking his disciples aside and explaining the parables he was using. At the end of a long day of teaching, when evening had come, Jesus said to them, "Let us go over to the other side."

Two Types of Beliefs

Bible scholars have given various explanations for this decision. Some have suggested that Jesus had grown physically weary and needed to withdraw and rest. This is certainly true because we're told that He fell asleep as they traveled in the boat to the other side of the lake. Other Bible teachers believe that Jesus wanted to take His teaching to another geographical and social sphere, and His primary motive was to expand His ministry and to reach out to other audiences. However, I want to suggest that His primary reason for instructing the disciples to cross the lake at this point was because Jesus knew that there was a storm coming, and that His disciples needed this storm to expose their fears and to teach them at a deep experiential level that they were in His protective care.

This suggestion may be shocking to some readers, and it may seem inconsistent with the character of Christ that He would deliberately send them into a storm to teach them a lesson. However, this is exactly what happened in John 11 when Jesus was informed that His friend Lazarus was sick and dying. In verse 6 the Scriptures say that, "When therefore He heard that he was sick, He stayed then two days longer in the place where He was." Jesus told his disciples that "This sickness is not unto death, but for the glory of God," (v.4) and He knew that

Lazarus was going to die and be raised from the dead. He also knew that many of Lazarus' friends would be deeply saddened and grieved by his death, but He delayed His trip to Bethany so that Lazarus would die, because He knew that they needed this experience to fully learn to trust Him.

The same is true in Mark 4. Jesus told His disciples to cross over to the other side because He knew that a storm was coming, and they needed that storm to expose their fears and teach them experientially what they only knew at an intellectual or surface level. The Lord knows that we need deep inner truth in addition to surface beliefs in order to fulfill the missions that He has given each of us to fulfill.

This distinction between intellectual, surface beliefs and deeply embedded experiential beliefs is very important, and can be seen clearly in Mark 9, where a man brought to Jesus his son, who had convulsions due to a spirit in him that often threw him into fires and into the water to destroy him. This desperate father said to Jesus in v.22, "If You can do anything, take pity on us and help us!" Jesus said to him, "'If You can!' All things are possible to him who believes" (Mark 9:23). But the boy's father then cried out and said, "I do believe; help my unbelief" (v.24).

This man was experiencing what we all experience at times. We believe that God loves us, or we believe that He is able to provide for us and protect us, but we experience overwhelming fears and doubts in spite of these beliefs. Intellectually we know that God is loving and powerful, but from our past experiences we have fears and doubts that control us. The Lord is able to replace our deep inner lies with truth, so that we know the truth and feel peaceful and calm in the midst of storms. When He does this we will not only know intellectually that God loves us, but we will also feel loved at an emotional level. We will not only know intellectually that "my God shall supply all [my] needs," but we will also feel peaceful when we are threatened with the loss of our job or our insurance.

I have never gone sky-diving, but when I was much younger I had the desire to do so. Now, I believe that sky-diving is a safe sport when the individual is properly trained and follows the guidelines taught by the sky-diving instructors, and I have personally witnessed many sky-divers and have seen them on television many times. I have never observed a time when someone was injured or died from sky-diving. However, if you were to take me up in an airplane to parachute, I know that I would experience strong emotional fears, because I have intellectual or surface beliefs that it is safe, but my experiential beliefs that it is not safe would control my emotions. I know how it feels to fall off the roof of a house, and this experience would show what I really believe, and cause me to be fearful if I was taken up into a plane to go skydiving.

God wants us learn truths intellectually, but He knows that we need experiential beliefs (a term coined by Ed Smith in *Beyond Tolerable Recovery*) in Him to deal with the challenges He brings our way. We also need experiential beliefs so that we can trust Him during these times and experience the inner peace that He offers. Many believers know a great deal about God; they have studied the Scriptures, they have memorized many verses, and they have good biblical and doctrinal knowledge, but these are all surface beliefs and intellectual knowledge. In order to resist temptations and be fruitful and victorious in our Christian lives, we also need to have our deep inner minds renewed so that our experiential beliefs match our intellectual beliefs. Jesus' disciples had received intellectual knowledge, but needed more experiential knowledge of Him to be able to endure the trials He would be taking them through. So, in Mark 4 Jesus tells His disciples to cross over to the other side knowing that a storm is coming.

Circumstances Are Not the Cause of our Fears

Mark 4:37 tells us that "there arose a fierce gale of wind, and the waves were breaking over the boat so much that the boat was already filling up." The disciples became alarmed as the storm increased its strength, but they apparently waited a long time before they finally went to the Lord, who was sleeping, and woke Him up. Their response makes it clear that they were very stirred up about the storm and upset that Jesus was sleeping through it: "Teacher, do You not care that we are perishing?" (v.38)

However, it is clear from this passage that the storm was not the cause of their fears. If the storm had been the cause of their fears then they would all have been upset, but there was one person in the boat who was not upset: the Lord. He was sleeping soundly and was not worried about their safety even when the boat began to fill up with water. He was at complete peace while His disciples were in a panic.

This illustrates an important principle: storms are not the cause of our fears, and external circumstances are not the true source of most of our negative emotions. This is a difficult principle for many people to accept, because it seems that other people and external circumstances cause our bad feelings. When someone criticizes us or treats us in an unkind or uncaring manner, we feel badly, and those feelings seem to come from them. Or if we lose our job and suddenly feel anxious about our future, it seems that these circumstances are the cause of our feelings of anxiety.

There are, indeed, some circumstances that create negative feelings such as sadness, disappointment, righteous anger and grief that are fact-based and not belief-based. These feelings have been discussed in previous chapters and are a natural response which normal people will experience. But the vast majority of negative feelings that people have are caused by lies they believe.

False Beliefs are the True Cause of our Fears

The Scriptures tell us that "perfect love casts out fear," (1 John 4:18) so the fear of the disciples was not based on truth. Notice the assumptions made by them in that simple statement made to Jesus, "Teacher, do You not care that we are perishing?" There are at least three lies contained in that statement.

The first lie they believed was that Jesus was just a good teacher. They were still addressing Him as "Teacher" in this instance, in spite of having witnessed miracles of healing. They did not understand yet that Jesus was the Son of God, the Creator, and so they were fearful that their lives could be taken by the storm. If they had fully known who Jesus was they would have been at peace, because they would have known that they were safe in His presence.

The second lie they believed was that Jesus did not care about them ("Do you not care...?"). This is a common reaction for us to have when we are in the midst of trouble. We quickly conclude that God doesn't care about us or He would not allow us to go through this difficulty. This is a lie. Sometimes God allows us to go through difficult experiences because He loves us and cares for us, and He knows that we need these experiences in order to learn deep inner truths about who He is. That is how we come to truly know God at an experiential level, by going through such experiences with Him. Jesus' disciples interpreted His sleeping as proof that Jesus really was indifferent to their plight, and did not care about them and their feelings.

The third lie His disciples believed was that they were going to perish ("we are perishing"). We have the benefit of knowing the end of the story and we know that they survived this storm and were used by God to begin the church. God had plans for them, and those plans could not be fulfilled if they were to die in this storm. The same is true for each believer; God has a plan for each of us, and nothing can end our lives until He has fulfilled his purposes for us in our lives. If the Lord chooses to end our lives there is nothing we can do to stop this, but if He still has other plans for us then He will preserve our lives, and nothing can harm us or prevent us from fulfilling His plan. As long as we are in the same boat as the Lord, metaphorically, we can rest assured that we are safe.

Only Jesus Can Give Us True Peace in the Midst of Storms

The Scriptures tell us in Mark 4:39 (KJV) that "being aroused, He rebuked the wind and said to the sea, 'Peace, be still.'" And the wind immediately died down and it became perfectly calm, and Jesus asked the disciples why they were so fearful and why they had so little faith. Jesus simply rebuked the winds. With three simple words, "Peace, be still," the storm and winds were calmed and they immediately became very still, just as David descrubed in Psalm 23:2, "He leadeth me beside still waters"(KJV).

What a picture that is of the power of God and what God wants to do in our lives! He wants us to be at peace even in the midst of storms, resting in the assurance that He is always in control, and knowing that everything that happens to us is designed by Him to accomplish His purposes. This kind of peace is something that only Jesus can bring into our lives. When we are stirred up and restless, the voice of Jesus can bring complete peace into our hearts with just a few words of truth.

No matter what the situation is, God can bring peace into our hearts when He whispers words of truth into our minds. Like the hymn "He Keeps Me Singing" says, "Jesus whispers sweet and low, 'Fear not, I am with thee; peace, be still.'" Others can sometimes bring words of healing and comfort to us, but no one can bring comfort to us like Jesus, through the Holy Spirit.

As a mental health counselor I tried for 25 years to talk Christians out of their bad feelings. I used the Scriptures and prayed with them and told them how to stand on the truths in God's Word and sometimes it seemed to help for a short while. But it never lasted long; they would eventually fall back into their former thinking and feelings. I was very discouraged, and felt helpless in dealing with such emotional issues, until I learned that Jesus is able to bring truth to people in a way that gives lasting comfort.

The truth is that only Jesus is able to set people free. Only Jesus is able to give us peace in the midst of storms. Jesus said, "If therefore the Son shall make you free, you shall be free indeed" (John 8:36). All of the mental health training and experience that I had did not enable me to set people free, but as I have learned to lead them to listen to Jesus, He sets them free and brings lasting peace into their hearts. He is able to speak directly into the minds of individuals and to change the experiential lies that are embedded in their memories. Men cannot do that, but the Lord can.

Summary of Principles for Dealing with Belief-based Emotions

When we are facing difficult circumstances and stress in our lives, it is very helpful to keep these four principles in mind so that we can understand what God is trying to do in our lives, and so that we can have our minds renewed. First, realize that it is your experiential beliefs that are controlling your emotions. Second, recognize that the "storms" and stressors in your life are not the true source of your emotional stress. Third, recognize that the stressors expose the lies you believe so that God can use this as an opportunity to renew your mind. And fourth, learn to pray for the Lord to bring you truth to set you free from your strong emotions. As you learn to listen to the Lord and hear His truth in your heart, your mind will be renewed and you will be able to remain calm and make wise decisions about what you should do in your difficult circumstances.

All of us experience stress in our lives. We all have storms that come into our lives, and the Lord allows those storms to come into our lives to expose the lies we believe, so that He can replace them with His truth. The Lord has given us His Holy Spirit whom He called "the Spirit of Truth," and promised that "the truth will set you free," but we have to be quiet and listen to the still small voice of God as he speaks to us.

The basic principle for dealing with negative belief-based feelings is what I like to call the James 1:5 principle, which will be described more fully in the next chapter. This simple principle will be applied in the remaining chapters to the seven emotions of fear, loneliness, helplessness, hopelessness, shame, defilement, and hurt.

May God help each of us to learn to pray without ceasing, to learn to cast all our burdens upon Him, and to learn to do as the Scriptures tell us, "Be still, and know that I am God" (Psalm 46:10, KJV). He is the Wonderful Counselor and He wants us to live in a state of constant dependence upon Him, so that we can learn experientially how "the peace of God, which surpasses all comprehension, will guard your hearts and your minds in Christ Jesus" (Philippians 4:7).

CHAPTER 7

Feelings of Fear and Anxiety

One of the phrases repeated most often in the Scriptures is the phrase, "Do not be afraid" or "Do not fear." In the 23rd Psalm David said, "Even though I walk through the valley of the shadow of death, I fear no evil; for Thou are with me." The Lord Jesus Himself told His disciples, "Let not your heart be troubled, nor let it be fearful" (John 14:27). But the apostle John summarized it nicely in 1 John 4:18 when he said "perfect love casts out fear." There is no doubt that the Scriptures consistently teach us that we do not need to be afraid, and yet fear is one of the greatest struggles of Christians today. And it comes in a wide range of forms.

Forms of Fears

One mature Christian woman had a phobia of wasps that resulted from a childhood experience in which she was trapped in a shed while being stung by a swarm of wasps. This did not generally interfere with her life in a significant way, but did occasionally cause embarrassment when a wasp flew through a room and she had been known to dive under a table. Another Christian woman had a fear of driving that was so debilitating that she sometimes crawled on her hands and knees to the car when it was time to drive to church.

One Christian man was so terrified of water due to a childhood experience that he refused to submit to believer's baptism. A young Christian man sought counseling because of some panic attacks he had begun to experience that prevented him from being able to drive a vehicle for awhile. Other individuals have a fear of the dark, a fear of test taking, or a fear of public speaking that may not interfere greatly with their life, but does hinder them from some social or recreational activities.

Some people just worry chronically about their children, about their health, or about their finances. Then there are individuals who have chronic generalized anxiety that interferes with their daily functioning and may prevent them from being able to function on a job. Many musicians and performers have some form of performance anxiety that interferes with their performance and may disrupt a promising career. And then, there are many individuals who have panic attacks or have suffered significant life traumas, and have a form of post-traumatic stress disorder which can destroy their social life and keep them in emotional bondage for their entire life.

All of these are forms of fears that the Lord wants to remove. They are all belief- based emotions that were acquired from root-cause events that deeply implanted false beliefs in the mind of the individual. The Lord wants to renew the minds of believers, and bring truth to all of the underlying beliefs that cause our fears.

The Still Small Voice of God

In his book *The Purpose-Driven Life*, (2002, Zondervan) pastor Rick Warren tells the story of a missionary who was retiring and returning to his home in the United States after 30 years of service as a missionary in Africa. It happened that he was on the same ship as the President of the United States, and as their ship pulled into the New York harbor there was a large crowd and a military band waiting for the President's return from a two-week trip to Europe. As the missionary observed the fanfare and excitement of the President's return to his homeland after a two-week absence, he began to feel depressed and saddened that there was no party to welcome him home after spending 30 years serving the Lord in a foreign country.

While experiencing these feelings he began to complain to the Lord in prayer, and suddenly the thought came into his mind, "My child, you are not home yet." With that thought his spirits lifted and the depressed feelings left him. That truth set him free from his depressing emotions instantaneously, and he was not troubled again with these thoughts.

This type of experience is very common among Christians from various church backgrounds, who can give an example of something similar that has happened in their lives, when some insight from the Lord gave them comfort and peace in the midst of difficult circumstances. It is an example of what is often referred to as "the still small voice of God" that brings comfort and peace to believers when they pray to the Lord. Many of the great hymns of faith make reference to such experiences, such as the hymn "He Keeps Me Singing." The first stanza of this song says, "There's within my heart a melody. Jesus whispers sweet and low, 'Fear not, I am with thee, peace, be still, In all of life's ebb and flow.'" "Jesus whispers sweet and low" is a reference to the quiet voice of God that brings His comforting truths to us in times of need.

This truth has its roots in the Old Testament but is illustrated in the lives of believers in the New Testament as well. The apostle James used the Old Testament prophet Elijah to illustrate some principles of effective prayer in James 5:16-18. The incident in this passage includes one of the most incredible displays of supernatural power ever seen, when the prophet Elijah confronted the ungodly prophets of Baal in 1 Kings 18 and God sent fire down from heaven to consume the offering that Elijah presented to Him. Elijah then seized the false prophets of Baal and slew them at God's command, and then prayed for God to send rain to end the three-and-a-half years of drought. James uses this example of Elijah's powerful prayers to teach us that "The effective prayer of a righteous man can accomplish much" (James 5:16).

However, Elijah "was a man with a nature like ours" (James 5:17). He became very fearful of king Ahab and queen Jezebel, who were so enraged that they swore to kill him within a day.

Elijah hid himself in a cave, pleading to God for his life. While awaiting God's word to come to him, the Scriptures state that a strong wind came, but God was not in the wind; and an earthquake came, but God was not in the earthquake; then a fire came, but God was not in the fire. Then we're told in 1 Kings 19:12 that God spoke to Elijah in a "still small voice" (KJV) or as the "sound of a gentle blowing" (NASB). Christians of virtually all denominations recognize that sometimes God speaks to us through his Holy Spirit in such a "still small voice." Some people describe this as a nudge or "tugging" experience when the Holy Spirit prompts us to do something. God's primary means of speaking to believers today is through the Word of God, but the Holy Spirit still speaks to us, when we listen, through this "still small voice."

The prophets of the Bible sometimes heard an audible, direct voice when God spoke to them, such as when God first spoke to the young prophet Samuel. Samuel did not recognize the voice of God initially but thought the priest Eli had called him, so he went to Eli, who recognized that God was speaking to Samuel. Paul heard the direct voice of God while on the Damascus road, and Moses spoke directly with God on Mount Sinai. Although God seldom speaks with an audible voice to believers today, He often speaks with a "still small voice" to our inner thoughts if we will learn to pray effectively and to recognize and listen to God's voice. The problem is that many believers hurriedly cry out to God and present their petitions to Him, but do not wait quietly for God to respond. They fail to follow the Scripture that says, "Be still, and know that I am God" (Psalm 46:10, KJV). King David, in contrast to most believers, spent time both crying out to God and listening to the Lord, who as a result brought truth and comfort to him as seen repeatedly throughout the Psalms.

During Emotional Healing Prayer, the prayer minister guides the process and teaches the ministry recipients how to pray for specific truths once their deep inner lies are revealed. He will ask permission to pray for them, and then instruct them to listen quietly and report any thoughts that enter their minds immediately after the prayer. I was interviewing a 12-year-old boy who had just been admitted into a group home for boys, and during our first session together, I asked him a routine counseling question—had he ever had any suicidal thoughts? He replied that he had, so I asked him when he had had these thoughts. To my complete surprise, he stated that he had had suicidal thoughts on the previous day. He said he had thought about killing himself because his mother had promised to visit him and had never showed up, so he felt unloved and unwanted. I asked him if he wanted to get rid of these thoughts and feelings, and he said he did, so I asked his permission to pray for him.

Thinking that he had probably had these feelings previously I prayed, "Lord, would you take him to the source of these feelings and his beliefs that he is unwanted and unloved?" Initially he was distracted so he asked me to repeat this, which I did, and I asked him to just listen quietly and report to me any thoughts or memories that came to his mind. I prayed for him again and he suddenly said, "I just got something. He said that someone does love me; God loves me." I replied "Okay, anything else?" He hesitated a few seconds and then said, "I just got something else. He said 'You're going to be okay. Your family loves you.'" I again said, "Okay. Lord, is there anything else that you want him to know?" He hesitated a few more seconds and then said, "Wait, I just got something else. 'Your brothers and sisters love you too. Don't hurt yourself.'" No other thoughts came to him so I asked him how he felt and he said that he felt calm. I asked him to try to feel the negative feelings he had had before when he felt like harming himself and he could not stir up those feelings. The depressed feelings were gone and the suicidal thoughts never returned. They were based upon his beliefs that he was unloved and unwanted, and when the truth came into his mind during prayer, it set him free from the painful feelings of depression.

Asking for Wisdom from God

I like to describe this as the "James 1:5 principle." James 1:5 says, "if any of you lacks wisdom, let him ask of God, who gives to all men generously and without reproach, and it will be given to him." W. E. Vine describes "wisdom" in his *Expository Dictionary of New Testament Words* (1981, Revell, p.221) as "having insight into the true nature of things." I like that definition, and it illuminates for us what this Scripture means. When the Lord brings truth into our minds about a matter, He gives us a fresh perspective and understanding of our lives and that new perspective gives us peace. In other words, when we are able to see our problems and circumstances through His eyes, we will have peace. And so, it is appropriate, whenever we are struggling emotionally, to go to the Lord in prayer and ask for "insight into the true nature of things." That is wisdom and we are promised that if we ask for His wisdom, He will grant it to us, if we are asking in faith and do not doubt.

Throughout my Christian life I have often prayed for wisdom. As a high school student I remember sometimes praying for God to help me pass a test. Sometimes I believe He helped me remember what I needed to know, but other times He did not because I had not diligently studied for the exam. I have often prayed for wisdom into God's specific will for me as to whether I should accept a particular job or buy a particular house, and I believe that He usually guided me in those decisions. But I rarely asked for His "insight into the true nature of things" when I was upset. More often I asked Him to remove the obstacle or person who appeared to be the source of my emotional distress. The principle that I now see in this Scripture is that we should be in the regular practice of taking our emotional burdens to the Lord, and rather than asking Him to simply remove them and change our circumstances, asking for His "wisdom" and truth so that we can face our circumstances with calmness and peace.

Praying with a Prayer Partner

Discernment is needed when praying for God's wisdom, and if you are a young believer it is strongly recommended that you find a mature Christian prayer partner to pray with you for emotional healing, so that they can help you determine the source of the thoughts that come to you as you pray. In the case of the 12-year-old boy it was obvious to me that the thoughts he was having after my prayer were consistent with biblical truths. But sometimes prayer recipients have intrusive thoughts that are clearly not from the Lord, such as "It's true; you are alone and unwanted. No one cares about you." Our thoughts can come from God, from ourselves, or from the enemy. The thoughts that enter your mind after you pray for God to bring you truth are generally thoughts from God. However, sometimes they may be your own thoughts, and sometimes you may have thoughts that are planted in your mind by the enemy. You need to select a prayer partner who is a mature Christian with a good grasp of the Scriptures that enables them to discern whether the thoughts coming to you are consistent with the Word of God. If they are not, either you are deceiving yourself with your own mind or the enemy is attempting to deceive you with a lie.

One of the most telling indicators of whether the thought is from God, is what results from the insight or truth. It should bring you increased peace, although you may also find momentary peace by simply suppressing your thoughts or numbing yourself, and Satan is more than happy to help you do that so that he can keep you in bondage. However, if you have truth in your mind, you will find that the thought brings you immediate peace in that memory. It is helpful at times to ask yourself, "How does that make me feel?" after you receive an insight from the Lord. Isaiah 55:9-12 says

> "For as the heavens are higher than the earth, So are My ways higher than your ways, And My thoughts than your thoughts. For as the rain and the snow come down from heaven, And do not return there without watering the earth, And making it bear and sprout, And furnishing seed to the sower and bread to the eater; So shall My word be which goes forth from My mouth; It shall not return to me empty, Without accomplishing what I desire, And without succeeding in the matter for which I sent it. For you will go out in joy and be led forth with peace."

88

JIM GARDNER

This Scripture is literally fulfilled during prayer ministry sessions as the prayer partner or prayer minister prays for truth, then God speaks His truth into the mind and heart of the recipient, and it accomplishes God's purposes and brings peace. Observing how God speaks truth into the minds of others and brings immediate results and peace during a prayer session is exciting, and brings reassurance that God is indeed present and working in your life. God's thoughts bring peace, but our thoughts do not.

If you express a thought that your prayer partner recognizes to be blatantly unscriptural or inconsistent with the Scriptures, it is helpful for them to ask you, "Where do you think that thought came from?" Sometimes you recognize that it is a thought from the enemy and you can simply reject it. If you do not, you can pray for God to reveal the source of that thought, and then be able to discern whether the enemy is the true source of the thought. A prayer partner can also help by using his authority in Christ to send the spirit away and then continue the prayer session.

Three Ways of Receiving Truth

When God speaks through the still, small voice, the truth may come in one of three ways. The first and most common form of truth is when the prayer recipient has a clear, distinct thought that occurs to him, as in the example given earlier of the 12-year-old boy. Many people will describe this experience by saying "I heard the Lord say..." but they don't hear anything through their ears; it's simply a thought that immediately occurs to them.

The psalmist expressed this type of experience in Psalm 20:6 where he says, "Now I know that the Lord saves His anointed; He will answer him from His holy heaven." In Psalm 18:6 he wrote, "In my distress I called upon the Lord, And cried to my God for help; He heard my voice out of His temple, And my cry for help before Him came into His ears." The remainder of the psalm describes the Lord's answer and contains many truths that the Lord brought to his mind to comfort and strengthen him. The same experience can occur for believers today if they are willing to listen to the voice of the Lord.

The second way in which God brings truth is through a visual image. One woman, for example, after remembering a traumatic memory and feeling all alone and abandoned by her family, reported that she was picturing Jesus walking towards her and then holding her hand. This made her feel loved, and reassured her that she was not alone. It was a visual thought but it had the same calming effect upon her as if she had had a thought enter her mind.

A biblical example of a visual truth can be found in 2 Kings 6:8-23 in the life of the prophet Elisha. God spoke supernaturally to the prophet and many times warned him when Israel's enemies were about to attack. He passed these warnings on to the king of Israel. The king of Syria became enraged because he believed that there must be a spy among them who was forewarning the Israelites of their planned attacks. One of his servants, however, explained that the prophet Elisha was able to tell the Israelite king each planned attack. Upon hearing this, the Syrian king gave orders for his men to go to Dothan to capture Elisha.

He sent a large army with horses and chariots to surround the city, and early the next morning when Elisha's attendant went outside he saw that the Syrian army had surrounded the city and cried out in despair, "Alas, my master! What shall we do?" (v.15) Elisha tried to calm him by telling him the truth. He said, "Do not fear, for those who are with us are more than those who are with them." These words, although they were very true, were not very comforting to the attendant, so Elisha then prayed, "O Lord, I pray, open his eyes that he may see." The Scriptures then tell us that "the Lord opened the servant's eyes, and he saw; and behold, the mountain was full of horses and chariots of fire all around Elisha." God's truth was shown to this servant visually in this instance.

The third way in which God speaks is through a quiet realization of truth that enters the mind. Sometimes this occurs without even a distinct thought; the recipient just reports that he feels more calm. When you ask him why he is calm he will explain the reasons for the new-found calm, and these reasons are the thoughts that the Lord has brought into his mind.

Discerning the Lies

When the prayer minister prays for a recipient, it is also essential that he recognize that there are underlying lies behind the recipient's distress. Elisha knew that his attendant's distress was not caused by the Syrian armies; it was due to his lack of spiritual perception and truth. He simply prayed for God to open his servant's eyes because he knew the attendant was reacting in fear based upon the lies he believed. He believed they were outnumbered until God showed him the heavenly forces that were on their side. When we minister to others we must likewise discern the true source of emotional pain of our recipients, which is the false beliefs they hold. The Lord desires for us to have peace, but He sends His peace only after the purposes have been fulfilled for which He sent the troubling circumstances, namely, that we have our minds renewed. If we do not identify the underlying beliefs that are the source of our distress He will not generally provide us the truth we need. When we identify the lies and receive truth, our minds are renewed.

This story of Elisha illustrates a very important principle of healing prayer. God gives us His peace by opening our eyes to see the truth when we pray for one another. It is the truth that sets us free from our anxieties, but sometimes it requires the assistance of a third party to pray for us to have our eyes opened, so that we can see the truth. As God's truth illuminates our minds and removes the darkness and the falsehoods, we are suddenly filled with the peace of God, even in the midst of storms. This is why the apostle Paul prayed for the Christians at Ephesus, "I pray that the eyes of your heart may be enlightened" (Ephesians 1:18).

Many Christians pray fervently for God to change their circumstances when they are in distress, and they feel disappointed when God does not "answer" their prayer. But they fail to realize that God allows difficult circumstances in their lives so that their internal beliefs will be exposed and they can be set free of them. Their prayers would be more effective if they were to recognize that their fears and emotional distress are mostly caused by the deep-seated lies they believe, and pray for God to take them to the source of their feelings and then to give them His peace.

Elisha did not first pray for God to destroy the Syrian armies. He prayed instead for the Lord to open the eyes of his attendant so that his fears and despair would be removed. Only after the servant's eyes were opened and he was able to see the truth did Elisha pray for God to defeat the Syrians. He knew that the emotional despair of the attendant was clear evidence that he was being controlled by false beliefs which needed to be replaced by God's truth. In this case God used a visual image to impart His truth, so that the servant would realize the situation was not hopeless and that God was in total control.

Notice how this process involves the Holy Spirit, the Word of God, and prayer. The Word of God must be used by the prayer minister to guide him to discern whether the thoughts are from God or not; the Holy Spirit is guiding the whole process and bringing truth; and prayer is the means by which we seek God's truth. These three elements are the same three elements that have been used by Christians for centuries, but in Emotional Healing Prayer they are used in a manner different than is generally practiced today. The primary difference is in how the Lord speaks to our minds as we pray specifically for His truth regarding our beliefs, rather than praying for a change in circumstances.

Beliefs Underlying Our Fears

A young Christian man came to me for counseling regarding a number of concerns. One of his concerns was a panic attack he experienced one day while driving down an interstate highway in his city. The weather was stormy, and he was hurrying to get home when he was suddenly overcome with anxiety, and had to pull his car to the side of the road. He could not see any reason for this reaction, and after a short period of time his fears subsided so that he was able to continue driving home. However, he continued to have more anxiety attacks and sought help to overcome this irrational fear.

I asked him if he would be willing to remember how he felt that day and try to identify the source of his feelings and he stated that he was. I prayed and asked the Lord to give him the grace and courage to remember when he first felt this way. He quickly recalled a time a few years earlier when he was involved in a car accident in which the car he was in flipped over and he was hanging upside down. He stated that he felt very fearful while he hung there and he thought he was going to die. I asked him to focus on that thought and to allow himself to think those thoughts and feel those feelings. I prayed a simple prayer and asked the Lord to bring His truth to this young man. He told me that the thought came to his mind that it was over, the thought was untrue, and that God had protected him and prevented him from being harmed. He remembered how God had sent a bystander to help cut him out of his seat belt and free him from the car without serious physical injury occurring.

After praying and having these truthful thoughts come to his mind he stated that he was calm and no longer felt any fear. When I asked him to try to stir up the fears again by thinking about the accident and how frightening it was, he was unable to stir up the fears again. The thoughts had been replaced by the Lord with the truths that he was okay, he was not going to die, and the Lord was protecting him. When he was encouraged to think about the original panic attack that occurred while he was driving, he was unable to stir up those fears also. They had been removed by replacing the false beliefs with the truth about the root-cause events behind his fears.

The Root Lies Behind Fears

There are certain beliefs that usually occur when we become fearful. Some of the most common ones are listed below.

- Something bad is going to happen.
- He or she is going to hurt me.
- They are going to return and hurt me again.

- I am going to die.
- I am doomed.
- It's just a matter of time before something horrible happens.
- If I tell on them something bad will happen to me or my family.
- Someone evil is going to break in and hurt me.

When you or someone you are helping has fears they want to eliminate, it is often helpful to keep this list of beliefs in front of you to help you identify the specific underlying beliefs. Once you have identified these it is usually a simple matter of praying about them and asking the Lord for the truth, or asking what He wants this person to know. Once the Lord brings His truth to their mind they will instantly feel more calm and less fearful.

Four Steps to Emotional Healing

Although many believers report experiencing the "still, small voice of God," most do not experience it on a regular or predictable basis. However, Jesus promised that He would not leave us as orphans but that He would give us another "Helper" who would be with us forever, who would abide with us, be in us, give us His peace, and guide us into all truth (John 14:16-18, 26-27, 16:7-13). Clearly, the Lord was implying that the Holy Spirit was being given to us to guide us on a daily basis, which is why the Lord was able to say truthfully, "It is to your advantage that I go away; for if I do not go away, the Helper shall not come to you" (John 16:7).

The Holy Spirit is available to comfort us in all our afflictions (2 Corinthians 1:4) because He is available to us at all times. When we need comfort, He is available to give comfort through the truth that He brings to us. The Scriptures contain much truth and can bring great comfort when the truths we need are intellectual beliefs. However, when our emotional pain is rooted in deep inner beliefs and experiences from our past we may also need the Holy Spirit to provide comfort to us. Romans 8:26-27 tells us that the Spirit helps us when we do not know how to pray and "He...searches the hearts." There are four simple steps to Emotional Healing Prayer that generally result in the Holy Spirit's comforting truth being brought to the minds of believers.

First, try to identify your emotions in order to determine whether they are fact-based emotions or belief-based emotions. Our emotions appear to be directly connected in our minds to our deep inner beliefs which are often rooted in earlier experiences. Your emotions are a direct window to your true belief system and to your past, and as you focus on these feelings and allow yourself to feel them, your false beliefs surface as well. You may have suppressed your emotions for years and have never learned to express your feelings, so it may help to write down your feelings or seek the help of a friend or mature Christian to help you identify your true feelings.

The reason why it is important to discern your true emotions is because each emotion has a different set of beliefs underlying it, and if you pray about the wrong beliefs nothing happens. You may not have a good emotional vocabulary, but by asking what thoughts and beliefs are connected to your emotions you can discern what the true emotion is. Then when you pray for truth regarding your beliefs, the Lord is quick to provide the truth you need in order to have peace.

One time I was praying with a woman whose native language was French and who had difficulty expressing her emotions in English. I met with her several times and thought she was feeling rejected and hurt because her husband had left her for another woman. We prayed for truth pertaining to her false beliefs repeatedly but after several sessions nothing had happened so I reconsidered her emotions and finally considered that perhaps she was experiencing more grief than hurt. When I asked her if she felt grief and sadness at the loss of her husband she excitedly said, "Yes, yes, that's it. I feel grief at his loss." When we prayed about her grief and gave it to the Lord she suddenly felt her negative emotions leave and then she felt the peace of Christ enter into her heart.

The second step is to try to identify the "Root-Cause Events" of the emotions, because they generally come from earlier experiences. This can usually be accomplished as you answer the question, "Have I ever felt this way before?" and you may then go immediately to the source of the feelings. Since the Lord will not violate your free will and force you to remember something that you have suppressed and does not want to remember, it is often helpful to affirm in prayer that you are willing to go to the source and origin of your feelings. You may also find it helpful to pray and ask the Lord to give you the grace and courage to go to the source of your emotions before trying to remember the first time you felt this way.

Some Christians may react to this step, asserting that it sounds like the secular theory of Freud to assert that our feelings result from early life experiences. However, there is ample Biblical support for this notion when we consider the many direct Biblical statements that speak about the importance of childhood training (Proverbs 22:6) and that clearly state the importance of childhood experiences. In addition, there are many indirect biblical statements that speak about the importance of man's earliest beliefs, when we consider many of the Scriptural metaphors used repeatedly throughout the Scriptures. Perhaps the four most common metaphors that speak of this are the root metaphor (Luke 8:13), the springs of water metaphor (Psalm 1:3, Proverbs 18:4), the rock foundation metaphor (Matthew 7:24-27, and the heart metaphor (Mark 7:21). Each of these metaphors can be found frequently throughout the Scriptures and clearly imply the importance of deep, underlying beliefs that are "planted" early in the mind of individuals. Long before Freud emphasized the importance of early life experiences, King Solomon said, "Train up a child in the way that he should go. Even when he is old he will not depart from it " Proverbs 22:6). He also said, "A plan in the heart of a man is like deep water, but a man of understanding draws it out" (Proverbs 20:5). If we are going to be men and women of understanding we must look beneath the surface thoughts and feelings of people to identify their root causes. This was an important biblical truth long before Freud came along, and just because he came to recognize the importance of it does not diminish its importance or validity.

In the third step, you need to identify the deep, inner beliefs behind the disturbing emotions. This is often accomplished found by simply asking "why" questions and asking "how did that make me feel?" Asking these questions repeatedly until the underlying belief is identified will enable you to ascertain the specific belief that is underlying your negative feelings, and then to pray specifically for the truth that you need. A chart called the Root Beliefs Chart is provided at the end of Chapter 14 that may be helpful in identifying your underlying beliefs.

The fourth and final step is to simply pray to the Lord for wisdom, and ask Him to bring you the truth that you need to know. It is helpful when you are new to this process to listen quietly and record any thoughts that come to your mind. As you begin recording your thoughts, you need to use your knowledge of the Scriptures to discern whether the reported thought is from the Lord, from your mind, or from the enemy. If you are not knowledgeable of the Scriptures it is important that you pray with a mature believer who can help you discern the truthfulness of the insights that come into your mind.

Summary of the Steps for Dealing with Belief-based Emotions

1. Identify the true emotions that you are feeling (Psalm 139:23).
2. Identify the root cause events behind your emotions (Matthew 7:24-27).
3. Identify the deep inner lies creating the strong emotions (James 1:14).
4. Pray for God's wisdom and truth to replace the lies (James 1:5-8).

A story is told of a young man who applied for a job as a Morse Code operator at a time when the telegraph was the fastest method of long-distance communication. Answering an ad in the newspaper, he went to the office that was listed. When he arrived, he entered a large busy office filled with noise and clatter, including the sound of the telegraph in the background. A sign on the receptionist's counter instructed job applicants to fill out a form and wait until they were summoned to enter the inner office.

The young man filled out his form and sat down with the seven other applicants in the waiting area. After a few minutes, the young man stood up, crossed the room to the door of the inner office, and walked right in. Naturally the other applicants perked up, wondering what was going on. They muttered among themselves that they hadn't heard any summons yet. They assumed that the young man who went into the office had made a mistake and would be disqualified. Within a few minutes, however, the employer escorted the young man out of the office and said to the other applicants, "Gentlemen, thank you very much for coming, but the job has just been filled." The other applicants began grumbling to each other, and one spoke up saying, "Wait a minute, I don't understand. He was the last to come in, and we never even got a chance to be interviewed. Yet he got the job. That's not fair!" The employer said, "I'm sorry, but for the last several minutes while you've been sitting here, the telegraph has been ticking out the following message in Morse Code: "If you understand this message, then come right in. The job is yours." None of you heard it or understood it. This young man did. The job is his."

The same principle applies to us when it comes to prayer and receiving healing truth from the Holy Spirit. We must be willing to remember the root events that planted the lies in our minds, identify the underlying beliefs that are upsetting us, and then pray for wisdom as we are instructed to do in James 1:5. But we must also *listen* to the Lord and allow Him an opportunity to answer our prayers. You will know when the truth has come from the Lord, because it will set you free from the darkness and emotional bondage of the lie you were believing. As Jesus said in John 8:32, "you shall know the truth, and the truth shall make you free."

CHAPTER 8

Feelings of Loneliness and Abandonment

A couple came to me who were having marital problems. One of the wife's complaints was that when her husband became angry at her, he raised his voice at her and she became fearful that he was going to leave her. As she began talking about this she began to cry, so I asked her, "How does that make you feel when you begin talking about this?" She answered, "It makes me feel sad, and scared and lonely." So I asked her, "Would you be willing to let yourself remember the first time that you felt these feelings?" She said that she would, and I said a short prayer and asked the Lord to take her to the source and origin of her feelings.

The woman began to cry and she said that she had felt this way as a child when she was about six years old. She had been playing with a neighbor friend, and when she went home she was a couple of minutes late, and her father had locked the doors and wouldn't let her come inside. She knocked and knocked on the door and eventually he came to the door and yelled at her, telling her that she was late and she would just have to stay outside that night. She asked him what she should do and he told her that maybe she could go to the church down the street and find a place to sleep there, then he closed the door and locked her outside.

The little girl sat on the steps of her front porch and cried. She was frightened because it was getting dark and she didn't know what to do so she walked to the church down the street, but nobody was there. She sat down on the church steps and cried and cried, feeling frightened and all alone. It continued to get darker, and then she saw the figure of a man coming down the sidewalk in front of the church. As he got closer she eventually recognized him as the town drunk, who often was seen walking around town. When he got close to her he noticed that she was crying and he asked her what was wrong. The little girl told him what had happened and how her daddy had locked her out of the house because she was late coming home.

I asked this woman how she felt at that time while she sat there on the steps of the church, and she said that she felt really scared and all alone and unprotected. She cried again as she recalled the childhood incident, and I asked if I could pray for her about those feelings and beliefs. She gave me permission, and I prayed, "Lord, what do you want this little girl to know about this belief that she is all alone, unprotected, and unwanted?" I told her to just quietly listen to see if any thoughts came to her mind and she quickly said, "I just had the thought that I wasn't alone; God was with me all along. He was protecting me." I asked her if that felt true and she said it did.

She told me that when the town drunk heard what had happened he took her by the hand and walked with her back to her house and knocked on the door. When her father came to the door he was not happy to see the man or his daughter, but the man told her father that he shouldn't leave her outdoors at night and he needed to let her come in. Her father, still angry at her, reluctantly let her come in and told the man to leave. The little girl came in the house and ran upstairs to her room and the man went on his way. As the wife recalled this incident she began crying again and said, "That man was my angel. God sent him there to me to protect me. I was never really alone because God was with me."

The Lord's Experience

Feelings of loneliness and aloneness are some of the most powerful feelings that we can have, and we all feel them at times. The Lord Jesus experienced strong feelings of aloneness at Calvary and at the Garden of Gethsemane as he prayed to the Heavenly Father and said, "Father, if Thou art willing, remove this cup from Me; yet not My will, but Thine be done" (Luke 22:42). Jesus was already feeling alone because in His hour of need, when He was minutes away from being betrayed into the hands of His enemies to be crucified, when His Father was about to turn His back to Him as He bore our sins on His shoulders, His closest friends and disciples were all sleeping. And the Scriptures tell us in Luke 22: 43-45, "Now an angel from heaven appeared to Him, strengthening Him. And being in agony He was praying very fervently; and His sweat became like drops of blood, falling down upon the ground. And when He rose from prayer, He came to His disciples and found them sleeping from sorrow."

Jesus, our Wonderful Counselor, understands what it is like to be utterly and completely alone. It was this that caused Him, I believe, to sweat as it were "drops of blood" in the Garden of Gethsemane. It was this that led Him to pray, "If it is possible, let this cup pass from Me" (Matthew 26:39). It was the reason that He cried out on the cross, "My God, My God, why hast Thou forsaken Me?" (Matthew 27:46). All His friends had forsaken Him and fled for their lives, all His followers were gone, He was falsely accused and treated as a criminal and even His Heavenly Father turned His back on Him, to let Him die alone. In John 16:32 Jesus spoke of this coming moment when He said, "Behold, an hour is coming, and has already come, for you to be scattered, each to his own home, and to leave Me alone; and yet I am not alone, because the Father is with Me." But when He was crucified for us, even His Father abandoned Him and He was all alone. That's a sad, sad thing and a very painful thing to bear, but Jesus bore it for us.

The Scriptures tell us in John 19:30 that after He took the sour wine He cried out, " 'It is finished!' And He bowed His head, and gave up His spirit." And then when one of the soldiers pierced His side with a spear, "immediately there came out blood and water" (v.34). He didn't die from the wounds in His hands and feet or from suffocation like the two other men who were crucified with Him and had their legs broken. Many Bible teachers believe He died from intense sadness and loneliness and from a broken heart.

The Promise of the Lord

In the same way that the Lord Jesus was "acquainted with grief," He was also acquainted with loneliness and abandonment. And just before He entered into that very lonely hour, He worked hard to comfort his friends and disciples so that they would not feel alone. In John 14:18, Jesus said to them, "I will not leave you comfortless: I will come to you" (KJV). In the NASB it is translated, "I will not leave you as orphans; I will come to you." Shortly after that, in John 16:7-13, He again tells them that when He leaves He will send them the Holy Spirit, the Helper, the Comforter to be with them so that they would never be alone. And then we have the promise given to us in Hebrews 13:5 where the Lord tells us, "I will never desert you, nor will I ever forsake you," or as it is translated in the KJV, "I will never leave thee nor forsake thee." I understand that this is written as a triple negative in the Greek, so that it could accurately be translated, "I will never, never, ever leave you or forsake you!"

Isn't that a wonderful promise? The Lord knows how devastating and powerful these feelings of aloneness can be, and He promises us "I will always be with you." David said in Psalm 27:10, "For my father and my mother have forsaken me, but the Lord will take me up." Even your own parents may forsake you, but the Lord never will. That's the promise we have from God's Word. The prophet Isaiah said in 49:15, "Can a woman forget her nursing child, And have no compassion on the son of her womb? Even these may forget, but I will not forget you." So you will never be truly alone like the Lord Jesus was. We may feel alone at times, but the truth is that the Lord is always with us.

The feelings of aloneness and abandonment that the Lord felt were truth-based feelings, but when we feel them they are lie-based, because we are never truly alone like He was. Just like the little girl I described earlier, we are never really alone. The Lord was with her even when she felt so alone, and then the

Lord opened her eyes, as an adult, so that she was set free from the feelings of aloneness that had plagued her all of her adult life. When we feel abandoned, alone, or lonely the Lord wants to replace these lies with the truth that we are never alone because He is always with us.

Times of Loneliness and Abandonment

There are many occasions that lead individuals to feel alone or abandoned. One of the most common is the death of a spouse, or loss of a spouse due to divorce. Those who experience the death of their spouse or a divorce may have feelings of loss and grief, which was discussed in Chapter 1. It is a truth-based feeling that can be effectively removed when we give those feelings to the Lord and ask Him to carry them for us. But after the feelings of grief are eliminated there may remain some feelings of loneliness and/or abandonment that are lie-based feelings. The same is true for children who lose a parent due to death or divorce. They may have truth-based feelings of grief as well as lie-based feelings of loneliness and/or abandonment that will require the Lord's healing grace.

Many children also feel lonely when they move and leave their friends behind and have to build new relationships. It is sometimes very difficult to build new friendships, and they can experience strong feelings of loneliness and aloneness. One boy was traumatized when his family moved to a foreign country to become missionaries, and he was rejected and ostracized by the children in the new country, where he looked different than the other children and was teased and picked on. He developed deep feelings of rejection and loneliness that led to desperate attempts to feel better through drug abuse and friendships with others who felt like social outcasts.

Adoptive children are often afflicted with deep-seated feelings of loneliness and abandonment. These feelings are deeply embedded in early childhood experiences and memories, and must be exposed and removed through prayer to prevent the development of unhealthy behavior and relationship patterns. This pattern of dysfunctional behaviors is referred to in the mental health field as "Reactive Attachment Disorder" and is difficult to remove to enable the child to live a normal life. However, it does not require traumatic separation or abandonment for a child to develop strong feelings of loneliness. Sometimes children who grow up in normal Christian homes experience times of aloneness, and the enemy uses these occasions to plant destructive lies and seeds of loneliness. A sickly child may require hospitalization and this may implant feelings of abandonment or loneliness while he is separated from his parents. Or the child may become briefly lost or separated from his parents in a crowd, and this may implant deep separation anxiety or feelings of aloneness.

Another occasion that may stimulate feelings of aloneness is when young adults fail to find a marriage partner. They may feel alone, unprotected, and believe that they don't belong. Or they may simply feel a need for companionship and relationships, because it becomes increasingly difficult for single adults to relate to others when most of their friends are married and have a spouse and children to care for. When they attend church they may feel lonely when they have to sit alone in church and are never invited into the homes or lives of their married church friends. Churches should be alert to this need and open their hearts and homes to single adults. I believe it is a sin for a church to allow a single person to attend their church repeatedly and to have no one who will sit with them and help them feel welcomed into their fellowship.

One of the most vulnerable times in our lives is when we are experiencing significant times of sickness and death. When individuals are facing life-threatening surgery or illness they generally long for evidence that someone cares for them, and they are subject to feelings of loneliness. Christians who understand this or who have experienced this should reach out to those in their acquaintance who undergo serious surgical procedures and life-threatening circumstances. Pastors and church leaders who recognize this need have active ministries to shut-ins, nursing homes, and hospitals. No one wants to lie in the hospital under such circumstances without contact with others who understand their feelings and love them enough to visit them.

Several years ago I underwent triple bypass heart surgery to prevent a serious heart attack. I walked into the hospital with my wife for exploratory surgery to determine my medical needs and was advised to have immediate open-heart surgery to relieve the pressure to my heart of three blocked arteries. I consented to the procedure, and while I was waiting for the operating room and staff to prepare for surgery I was shuffled, in a half-conscious state, to a waiting area in the hospital basement for what seemed like hours. As I lay there I felt no fear of dying, but I had nothing to do but think about what could happen. Many things could go wrong during surgery, because this was a very serious surgical procedure in which I would be attached to an artificial heart while my heart was stopped and the doctor performed the bypass surgery. This could be my last time to see my family, but there I lay in the cold, dark basement of the hospital all alone. The more I thought of it the more alone I felt, and I began worrying about my family whom I realized I might never see again. It seemed to be a very cruel thing to leave me in such a lonely place totally void of human contact while I was waiting for the surgery that could end my life. Eventually, just before I was escorted into surgery my family was permitted to see me, and when they arrived my eyes were red with tears because I had been worrying about them and missing them.

After my surgery, I was again escorted to a dark, secluded area of the hospital basement. When I recovered consciousness I could see two or three other patients recovering from surgery spread out over a large, secluded basement area of the hospital. I had a tube running down into my throat that was extremely uncomfortable and prevented me from being able to swallow. My throat was dry and I could not speak to the nurse to ask for assistance. I couldn't turn over, swallow, or speak and the nurse stayed in an office most of the time so I couldn't signal for help. Eventually, he did come to check on me and I tried to speak with him and ask for some ice to relieve my discomfort, which he provided. Again, I waited for hours in a lonely, isolated room of the hospital with no human contact. When the doctor finally arrived and removed the tube from my throat it was a wonderful relief, but it was also relieving when I finally received some human contact and was able to see my family again.

Mother Theresa understood the vulnerability of humans when they are dying, and devoted her life to caring for the homeless who were on the verge of death, showing some human love and concern for those who had no one to care for them in their time of greatest need. What a wonderful example to all who claim to be Christians, to reach out to those who are sick, destitute of human relationships, and on the brink of death. I am convinced that it is a sin of great consequence to ignore the pain of those who are sick and dying, and those who do so may one day themselves be in such a state of need and find that no one will visit them in their last dying days.

Another circumstance that may provoke feelings of aloneness or loneliness is when individuals attempt to serve the Lord and find themselves all alone in their service. As a young child I remember my father giving me gospel tracts to pass out to passersby on the street while he played gospel songs over a PA system and preached to them about the Lord. I knew that he was doing a good thing and that he had good intentions. I even admired him for having the boldness to do this, but I was embarrassed and felt very alone in doing my part. Years later when I was in high school I did my best to be a good Christian witness and I sometimes carried my Bible to school with me so that I could read it during breaks. I tried to read my Bible at school during a study hall and I felt very alone and self-conscious as I tried to do this.

When I first learned about Emotional Healing Prayer I sought prayer ministry from the man who had introduced it to me. While I was dealing with some feelings of aloneness, he asked me when was the first time I could remember feeling similar feelings of aloneness and this high school memory came to my mind. He asked me how I felt in that high school classroom and I told him that I felt all alone and felt like I didn't fit in. The man prayed and asked the Lord what truth He wanted me to know about this belief that I was all alone. With my eyes closed I pictured that classroom and myself trying to read my Bible, and I glanced to my right and pictured the Lord Jesus sitting in the chair beside me, smiling at me. This brought tears to my eyes, and a strong assurance that I had never been alone, and that I pleased the Lord very much.

The Root Beliefs Behind Feelings of Aloneness

When we feel alone or abandoned, there are always root beliefs or lies that make us feel that way. These come in different forms, but the specific lies connected to our feelings need to be identified so that we can pray for the Lord to bring us the truth we need to be freed from these negative feelings. Some of the most common lies behind feelings of aloneness or abandonment are as follows:

- I'm all alone.
- No one understands me.
- No one cares.
- I've been abandoned.
- Even God has forsaken me.
- There is no one to protect me.
- I will always be alone.
- They will never come back for me.
- I don't belong.
- No one believes me.
- I don't matter.
- No one cares for me.

If any of these statements feels true to you while you recall a memory, it is probably one of the lies that is still controlling your life. At that moment you should pray to the Lord and ask Him what truth He wants you to know about that belief. Then wait quietly and see what thoughts come to your mind. Allow the Lord time to speak into your mind the truth that you are needing to receive in order to be free from the negative feelings of loneliness or aloneness that you feel.

Steps to Freedom from Feelings of Loneliness

The steps to finding freedom from lie-based feelings are very simple, although their application is sometimes complicated by hindrances that will be discussed in a later chapter. Generally speaking, the Lord will use His Holy Spirit to set you free and to comfort you as you follow the following four steps.

First, identify your present feelings. This may seem unimportant, but many people have learned to ignore or suppress their feelings for so many years that it is important to state this step. Before we can receive the truth we need from the Lord, we need to be honest with Him about our emotions. That means we need to quit denying our pain, quit suppressing our feelings, and be honest with the Lord about our emotions. One of the best examples of this in the Scriptures is the Psalmist David who often cried out to the Lord in times of emotional pain. He often experienced feelings of aloneness and cried out to the Lord, as he did in Psalm 102:7 when he said, "I lie awake, I have become like a lonely bird on a housetop." In Psalm 25:16 David said, "Turn to me and be gracious to me, for I am lonely and afflicted." So, do as David did and pour out your heart to the Lord, confessing your true feelings to Him and asking for His assistance. As part of this honest cry to God, let yourself feel those feelings in their fullness, because as you do so it brings your deeply buried lies to the surface so that the Lord can bring deep healing to your soul.

Second, identify the root-cause events behind these feelings. When young children are feeling hurt or lonely it may be the first time they have felt this emotion, and you can skip to the next step, but most of the time when adults feel lonely they have felt such feelings before. Sometimes the original experience of this emotion will come to your mind immediately and you will clearly remember the first time you felt this way. At other times it may be helpful to affirm to the Lord that you want to go to the source of your feelings, even if it is painful, because the Lord will not force you to go. He will wait until you are fully willing to go to the original source of these feelings. So, pray and ask the Lord to take you to the source of these feelings, to the first time you felt them. If you have another memory as an adult come to mind this is probably a secondary memory, but use that memory to further stir up your emotions, and then pray again and ask the Lord to take you to the original source. Once you discern what appears to be the root cause, allow yourself to remember how you felt in that memory.

Third, identify the false beliefs behind your feelings. You may find it helpful to use the list of root beliefs identified in the previous section of this chapter to help you identify the specific lies you were believing at the time when you first felt this feeling. If, for example, you believe you were feeling lonely or abandoned, then read through the list of common lies about loneliness and identify the statements and beliefs that "feel" true to you, even if you know they are not true. If they feel true, then they are probably lies that you believe that are still controlling you and your emotions.

The fourth and final step is to pray for God's wisdom and truth and listen quietly for the "still, small voice of God." Write down the thoughts that enter your mind and evaluate each to see that they are consistent with the Word of God. Most of the time the thoughts that come into your mind after praying for the Lord to bring you truth will be from Him, but they may be coming from your own mind or they may be coming from the enemy. The way to tell is to evaluate the thought with the Word of God. When the Lord brings His truth to your mind it will result in the peace of God in that memory. To test whether you have received full healing in that memory you may want to try to stir up the negative feelings you had previously, and nothing will happen once the healing is complete. You will feel complete peace and calm in that memory. There may be more thoughts the Lord wants to bring to you, so it is helpful to pray and ask Him if there is anything else that He wants you to know.

When you have completed these four steps you should find that the feelings of loneliness or abandonment you previously had are gone. There may be other memories that surface or other negative feelings remaining, and if so, then you can repeat the steps again to relieve each negative emotion that is connected to the memories that surface. After obtaining complete peace in these memories you can either stop, or ask the Lord to take you to any other place that He wants you to go at that time. If your circumstances require it you can simply stop and continue this prayer process when it is more convenient.

CHAPTER 9

Dealing with Feelings of Hopelessness

It has been estimated that approximately 12%, or about one in eight, of all Americans will experience an episode of clinical depression at some time in their lifetime of sufficient severity to warrant professional treatment. While a diagnosis of clinical depression involves a number of components, research has indicated that the central psychological component in the suicidal patient is hopelessness (Beck, Rush, Shaw, & Emery, *Cognitive Therapy of Depression*, Guilford Press, 1979, p. 1, 3).

A 1973 report by the National Institute of Mental Health on depressive disorders by Katz, Friedman, and Schuyler stated that 75% of all psychiatric hospitalizations are due to depression, and that during any given year 15% of all adults between the ages of 18 and 74 may experience significant symptoms of depression. These authors also suggested that treatment for these depressed individuals costs between 0.3 and 0.9 billion dollars per year (an amount that would be much higher now, even if only adjusted for inflation) and although antidepressant drugs are helpful in relieving people of depressed feelings, 35 to 40% of depressed people are not helped with their first trial of antidepressant drugs.

When an individual feels worthless and devoid of any hope of changing their feelings and enjoying life again, they eventually begin to entertain thoughts of ending their life in order to escape the pain of depression. Sometimes this occurs as a result of a lifetime of disappointments and unpleasant experiences, and sometimes it occurs when an individual is going through a particularly difficult set of experiences in their life. Christians are just as vulnerable as unbelievers to depression, in spite of the clear assertions in the Scriptures that we are never without hope because we have the God of hope in our lives. Consider the following example.

Pastor "Glenn" came to me due to severe depression and persistent suicidal thoughts that had continued for several months. His depression began when he went to church one Sunday morning and left his wife at home since she was feeling ill. When he returned from the service, however, he found her dead in her bed. She had committed suicide while he was preaching his sermon that morning. What exacerbated the situation for him was that he had had a child who had committed suicide a few years earlier, and now with a second member of his family having committed suicide he was overwhelmed with feelings of guilt and grief that he could not stop. He read Scriptures, quoted them to himself, tried to claim the promises of Scriptures, and tried to free himself from his feelings of guilt and failure, but he could not succeed in being rid of them..

Glenn then went to a psychiatrist who prescribed a heavy dose of antidepressants for him, but he found that he was one of the 40% of persons who do not benefit any from antidepressants. He continued to have strong, persistent feelings of depression and suicidal ideas, regardless of what he tried. He was committed to a psychiatric institution where he underwent electroconvulsive shock therapy (ECT), and upon his release he was referred to me for counseling. When I saw him his short-term memory had been disrupted by the ECT but he continued to have feelings of guilt and sadness from the loss of his wife.

I began to apply the prayer principles described in this book, and one by one the negative feelings began to dissipate. After a series of weekly sessions he was no longer having depressive feelings, and all of his suicidal thoughts had stopped so he chose to terminate treatment. When I last saw him, two years later, he was still doing well emotionally and spiritually and was no longer taking antidepressants. The Lord was able to heal him of his feelings of hopelessness and set him free from the emotional bondage he had experienced.

Biblical Examples of Depression

There are many examples of godly individuals in the Bible who experienced periods of depression and hopelessness. The apostle Paul told the Corinthian believers that he experienced so much affliction in Asia that "we were burdened excessively, beyond our strength, so that we despaired even of life"(2 Corinthians 1:8). There were many times that he was so persecuted, rejected, and afflicted that he despaired of life. In Philippians 1:23-24 he wrote, "I am hard-pressed from both directions, having the desire to depart and be with Christ, for that is very much better; yet to remain on in the flesh is more necessary for your sake." But he did not remain in this state of despair long; he found his hope in Christ. In 2 Corinthians 1:9-10 he stated, "indeed, we had the sentence of death within ourselves in order that we should not trust in ourselves, but in God who raises the dead; who delivered us from so great a peril of death, and will deliver us, He on whom we have set our hope." Again in 2 Corinthians 4:8-9 he wrote, "we are afflicted in every way, but not crushed; perplexed, but not despairing; persecuted, but not forsaken; struck down, but not destroyed."

Job was so afflicted that his wife implored him to curse God and die, but he refused to do so. He lost his house, his wealth, his children, his health, and his social standing, and then his friends came to him to try to persuade him that it was all his fault. In Job 19:9-10 he finally broke down and said, "He has stripped my honor from me, And removed the crown from my head. He breaks me down on every side, and I am gone; And He has uprooted my hope like a tree." Although Job was understandably depressed from his many afflictions, he never gave in to suicidal thoughts. When he could finally hold back no longer he began to accuse God of being unrighteous in afflicting him, until God spoke to him and rebuked him for his arrogance. Then Job realized his limited understanding and repented of his arrogance, and the Lord comforted him and restored his good fortunes to him.

In the Psalms David often expressed feelings of hopelessness. Like the apostle Paul he also suffered much opposition and conflict and was prone to feelings of despair when in the midst of serious difficulties. In Psalm 42:3-6 he wrote, "My tears have been my food day and night, While they say to me all day long, 'Where is your God?' These things I remember, and I pour out my soul within me...Why are you in despair, O my soul? And why have you become disturbed within me? Hope in God, for I shall again praise Him For the help of His presence." In Psalm 71:3-5 David tells us again the source of his hope: "Be Thou to me a rock of habitation, to which I may continually come; Thou hast given commandment to save me, For Thou art my rock and my fortress. Rescue me, O my God, out of the hand of the wicked, Out of the grasp of the wrongdoer and ruthless man, For Thou art my hope; O Lord God, Thou art my confidence from my youth."

Jeremiah was known as "the weeping prophet" because his ministry involved declaring the Word of God to a rebellious nation and king. Each time he declared the truth he was persecuted. He was mocked, ridiculed, cast into a prison, and then thrown into a muddy well where he was left to die. We can understand why he began to curse the day he was born: "Cursed be the day when I was born; Let the day not be blessed when my mother bore me!" (Jeremiah 20:14) In Lamentations 3 he wrote: "I am the man who has seen affliction...He has caused my flesh and my skin to waste away...I have become a laughingstock to all my people...And my soul has been rejected from peace; I have forgotten happiness. So I say, 'My strength has perished, and so has my hope from the Lord.'" (Lamentations 3:1-18). Then he finds hope again in the famous words in 3:21-23, "This I recall to my mind, Therefore I have hope. The Lord's lovingkindnesses indeed never cease, For His compassions never fail. They are new every morning; Great is Thy faithfulness."

The great prophet Elijah became depressed and despairing of life after his encounter on Mount Carmel when he destroyed the prophets of Baal. When he heard that Jezebel swore to kill him within a day he ran to Beersheba and then sat in despair under a tree. The Scriptures say in 1 Kings 19:4, "he requested for himself that he might die, and said, 'It is enough; now, O Lord, take my life, for I am not better than my fathers." But the Lord strengthened him and he took a forty day journey to Horeb, the mountain of God. It was there that he stood on the mountain while a strong wind tore the mountain apart, then a wind, an earthquake and a great fire came, but God did not speak to him yet. After these mighty forces had passed it was then that God spoke to Elijah in a "still, small voice" and gave him hope for the future.

Scriptures about Hopelessness

The Scriptures have a lot to say about hopelessness. Paul spoke of unbelievers in Ephesians 2:12 whom he described as "having no hope and without God in the world." In 1 Thessalonians 4:13 he spoke of those who were unbelievers and how they deal with death and grief saying, "that you may not grieve, as do the rest who have no hope."

Believers, on the other hand, are said to have the "God of hope" and need not ever feel hopeless. Consider the following examples:

"Now may the God of hope fill you with all joy and peace in believing, that you may abound in hope by the power of the Holy Spirit." Romans 15:13

"For it is for this we labor and strive, because we have fixed our hope on the living God." 1 Timothy 4:10

"This hope we have as an anchor of the soul, a hope both sure and steadfast." Hebrews 6:19

"Therefore, gird your minds for action, keep sober in spirit, fix your hope completely on the grace to be brought to you." 1 Peter 1:13

Regardless of how well we understand the biblical truth about hope, however, there is a big difference in knowing something intellectually and experientially. As discussed in Chapter 6, intellectual beliefs can be easily changed, but experiential beliefs are rooted in our past experiences and are much more difficult to change. It requires the work of the Spirit to dislodge those stubborn beliefs and to set us free from their power. Our job is to identify the underlying beliefs, and then to pray about them so that the Holy Spirit can uproot them from our minds.

Root Beliefs behind Hopelessness

When an individual is feeling hopeless and cannot overcome these feelings, it is because they have deeply embedded beliefs from prior experiences that create these feelings of hopelessness. Ask yourself if you are willing to try to remember the first time you felt those feelings of hopelessness. If you truly are, try to do so. If you have difficulty accomplishing this, then it may be helpful to pray and ask the Lord to take you to the source and origin of your beliefs. Some of the most common beliefs underlying feelings of hopelessness are as follows:

- There is no way out of this situation.
- This will just continue to occur; it will never end.
- Even God cannot help me get out of this situation.
- This situation is never going to change.
- I am completely hopeless.
- This is never going to end.

Overcoming feelings of Hopelessness

The steps for overcoming feelings of hopelessness are the same as those discussed previously for dealing with belief-based emotions. I will illustrate them by sharing an example of a young man who came to me one time for counseling.

"Jerry" was a young man who had been married for about two years and who had two young children. He was raised by his mother in a non-Christian home and had very little contact with his father as a child. Shortly after he got married he received

Jesus as his Savior, and determined to be a good father and husband. But life was difficult, trying to provide for the financial needs of his wife and children without any specialized training or job skill, and since his wife was pregnant and busy taking care of their two young children, he was responsible for all of their financial needs. His wife had some emotional insecurities that he had to deal with as well, and when he came for counseling he shared that he felt overwhelmed and incapable of being a good father and husband. He felt like leaving his wife.

As Jerry shared his feelings he broke down and began to cry. I asked him what he was feeling at that moment. "I just feel completely hopeless. I don't think I can do this. I'm just like my father who didn't have the strength to raise his family. I wanted to do better but I just can't handle it," he sobbed.

"Have you ever felt this way before?" I asked him. "When you focus on your feelings of hopelessness right now, can you remember the first time you ever felt this way?"

Jerry thought about this for a few seconds and then said, "Yeah, I remember feeling this way as a kid."

"Tell me what you remember about that experience," I responded.

"I remember I was in school and I was making poor grades, and my mother was scolding me and yelling at me because I was doing badly. I remember crying and thinking 'I just can't do this. It is too hard. I'll never be able to learn this.'"

"Would you mind if I prayed with you about this memory and this thought that it is hopeless and impossible for you?" I asked him. He nodded, so I told him to just focus on that memory and his feelings of hopelessness. I prayed, "Lord, what do you want Jerry to know in this memory? What is the truth that you want him to know about this belief that it is hopeless?"

Almost as soon as I had finished praying he stated that he had the thought that "I did learn what I needed to, and I passed all my classes."

"Just listen quietly, now, and see if any more thoughts come to you," I instructed him. "Lord, is there anything else you want Jerry to know?"

"I heard the thought in my head that the Lord helped me then to do what I needed to do, and He will help me now."

"Does that feel true to you to say that 'the Lord will help you to be a good father and husband'?" I asked him.

"Yes," he replied. "I am not my father; we're different people, and if I look to the Lord for strength, the Lord will help me do what I need to do."

Six years later when I saw that young man and remembered this time of prayer with him it thrilled me to see him continuing to raise his family, working hard, and being faithful to take his wife and their six children to church each week. I thank the Lord for setting him free from his feelings of hopelessness through the Holy Spirit. The enemy wants to steal, kill, and destroy but the Lord wants to set us free through His truth.

Four Steps to Freedom

The four simple steps to freedom from hopelessness can be seen in the example given above. Sometimes it takes many more sessions to expose all of the negative emotions that individuals have and see them set free from all their despair and hopelessness but the same basic steps are used. They are as follows:

1. Identify your feelings of hopelessness.
2. Identify the root events underlying your feelings of hopelessness.
3. Identify the root beliefs causing you to feel hopeless.
4. Pray for the Lord to bring truth to you about your beliefs that your situation or life is hopeless.

Using these simple steps you'll find, as I did with Pastor Glenn and this young man, that the Lord is able to restore your souls, renew your mind, and replace your despair and depression with hope. As the apostle Paul said in 2 Corinthians 1:9-10, God allows us to experience such times of difficulty so that we will learn that "we should not trust in ourselves, but in God who raises the dead; who delivered us from so great a peril of death, and will deliver us, He on whom we have set our hope. And He will yet deliver us."

CHAPTER 10

Dealing with Feelings of Helplessness

When "Sharon" went for counseling with her husband "Bill," she complained that he did not help her more. His job required him to travel often, and when he had recently gone on a trip, leaving her to take care of the children and his ill father alone, she felt overwhelmed and worn out from trying to get him to stay and help her. She was angry, and stated that she felt hurt, sad, abandoned, alone and unloved, even though she admitted that her husband was a wonderful Christian. Mostly, however, she felt overwhelmed with all of her emotions, and felt helpless about getting her husband to understand her needs and help her out more.

Our session began like this. "Would you be willing to focus on those feelings and try to remember the first time you felt similar feelings of helplessness?"

Sharon nodded and closed her eyes as I prayed, "Lord, would you take Sharon to the source and origin of these feelings of helplessness she is feeling?"

She began to cry as she remembered being a four-year-old child who lived with her grandmother in South America. Her mother left the country when she was one year old and moved to the United States, but she was unable to take Sharon with her so she left her in the care of her grandmother. Sharon had become very close to her grandmother and regarded her as her mother. Then at 4 years of age her grandmother explained to her that she was going to live with her real mother in the United States, but that she first had to go to another city to get a visa.

Through her tears Sharon described how alone and abandoned and frightened she felt during this time. She was sent to live with a bachelor friend of her grandmother's for a short while, and during this time an employee of the bachelor's began to sexually abuse her. Because she felt so helpless and so small she was unable to resist him. This abuse continued for about a year until she went to live with an aunt and then eventually received her visa and was sent to the United States to live with her mother.

Sharon cried heavily as she described the feelings she had during the sexual abuse. She said that she felt completely helpless because she was a small child and she needed someone to protect her. I prayed for her, "Lord, what is it that you want this little girl to know?" I instructed her to just listen quietly and report any thoughts that came into her mind.

Sharon began crying and said, "I'll never leave you or forsake you." Those first thoughts were clearly biblical thoughts from the Lord. "God was angry at that man," she continued. "He is my shield; He will protect me" she added.

Sharon explained that she was confused and in a very vulnerable state at that time. She felt sad and alone because her grandmother was not there with her and she missed her immensely. She felt unprotected, unloved, and all alone. I encouraged her to focus on those feelings and prayed again, "Lord, is there anything else that you want this little girl to know?"

She reported that she was picturing in her mind a large hand reaching down and lifting her up, which she described as the hand of God. Then she said, "He suffered through it with me. He is sorry that it happened and He wants to give me a big hug."

"Are you willing to let Him do that?" I asked, which she affirmed she was. "Go ahead and see if anything else happens," I instructed her.

"He is surrounding me and protecting me" Sharon reported. Those feelings were very comforting to her and she felt stronger and less fearful.

Sharon then experienced feelings of anger toward her parents for taking her away from her grandmother and making her live in the house with the man that molested her. I affirmed that her feelings of anger were valid, and then she decided that she did not want to be angry any more. After some more truth coming to her mind, she indicated that she no longer felt helpless in that memory. When we returned to the original feelings of anger at her husband, she stated that she was no longer angry at him because she knew he had to travel with his job, and she no longer felt overwhelmed and helpless.

Underlying Beliefs about Helplessness

Feelings of helplessness or powerlessness are very common with abuse victims and often underlie feelings of anger. As a child I remember having a recurrent dream in which I was running from someone who was much larger than me and trying to hurt me, and I was running against a very strong wind that prevented me from escaping. This dream was symbolic of my feelings as a small child that I was small and powerless in a world of evil people. Many people have similar beliefs.

While it is true that there are evil people in the world who are much stronger than most of us, the truth is that the Lord is able to deliver us out of their hand if we will learn to trust in Him.

The beliefs that are most frequently connected to these feelings are as follows.

- I'm weak.
- I'm overwhelmed.
- I'm helpless against him.
- I cannot do anything against him.
- I'm too small to do anything about it.
- I'm going to die.
- Everything is out of control.
- I'm trapped and there is no way out.

Biblical Examples of Helplessness

There were many times in the history of Israel when the Israelites were surrounded by their enemies and they felt helpless and overwhelmed. In 2 Chronicles 20:12 the king of Judah cried out to the Lord when he had a mighty army coming to invade their land and he said, "we are powerless before this great multitude who are coming against us; nor do we know what to do, but our eyes are on Thee." The Lord said to him, "Do not fear or be dismayed; tomorrow go out to face them, for the Lord is with you" (2 Chronicles 20:17). The next day the Lord delivered them without their having to fight. The people began singing and praising the Lord, and the enemy destroyed themselves, without any of the Israelites having to raise a finger in their own defense (2 Chronicles 20:22-30).

The first time Israel was surrounded by their enemies was when they had just left Egypt, and were rejoicing in their freedom when the Lord led them to the Red Sea to camp. There were mountains on two sides, the Red Sea was in front of them and the king of Egypt decided to chase after them from behind with his chariots and horses. Exodus 14:10 tells us that "the sons of Israel looked, and behold, the Egyptians were marching after them, and they became very frightened; so the sons of Israel cried out to the Lord." They were frightened because they were trapped, and defenseless against the well-armed soldiers of Egypt. They felt helpless. But notice what Moses said to them in Exodus 14:13-14, "Do not fear! Stand by and see the salvation of the Lord which He will accomplish for you today; for the Egyptians whom you have seen today, you will never see them again forever. The Lord will fight for you while you keep silent."

Of course we know the rest of the story. The angel of God moved the pillar of cloud from before them and placed it between the camp of Egypt and the camp of Israel. Then he told Moses to lift up his staff over the sea and God caused a strong wind to divide the sea and to dry the land so the Israelites could walk across on dry land. When the Egyptian army tried to chase them into the midst of the sea, the Lord closed up the waters again and drowned the entire army of Egypt without a single Israelite having to fight (Exodus 14:19-31).

With a God like that beside us we never need to feel helpless or fearful. As children most of us learned the words to the chorus "Jesus Loves Me."

Jesus loves me, this I know,
For the Bible tells me so.
Little ones to Him belong.
They are weak, but He is strong.

What a powerful truth that is, and it is something that every child and every adult needs to know in their mind and in their heart, because we all face circumstances at times that are beyond our strength and our abilities. And God wants us to know, in those times, that He is with us, and He will be our strength.

The Israelites should have learned an important lesson on the day that the Egyptians were drowned in the Red Sea, and should have come to realize that no matter what the circumstances, God was with them and nothing was impossible with God. However, when they arrived near the land of Canaan which God promised He was going to give to them, they panicked when they heard the report of the spies they had sent into the land, who told them that the people of the land were strong, the cities were well fortified, and there were giants living in the land. Joshua and Caleb, however, had confidence in the Lord and told them, "We should by all means go up and take possession of it, for we shall surely overcome it" (Numbers 13:30).

The other men who had gone into the land as spies frightened the people with their report by saying, "We are not able to go up against the people, for they are too strong for us...all the people whom we saw in it are men of great size...we became like grasshoppers in our own sight, and so we were in their sight" (Numbers 13:31-33). With those words the people of Israel felt overwhelmed and helpless and frightened, and they began to organize a revolt against Moses, deciding to return to Egypt where they felt protected by the king, even though they were severely persecuted. Joshua and Caleb tried to calm them and reason with them, telling them, "the Lord is with us; do not fear them" (Numbers 14:9). But the people prepared to stone them, so the Lord intervened, pronouncing his judgment that none of the adults then living in the tribes of Israel would enter the Promised Land (Numbers 14:10-38).

In a previous chapter we examined the incident in the life of Elisha when the Syrians attempted to capture Elisha because he was providing the king of Israel divinely given information about the plans of their enemies to ambush them. One morning when the attendant of Elisha went out of their house, he saw that a huge army with horses and chariots was circling the city and he panicked and cried out. Although Elisha was facing the same overwhelming odds and circumstances, he remained calm and did not feel helpless, because he knew the truth which he stated in 2 Kings 6:16, "Do not fear, for those who are with us are more than those who are with them." Isn't it amazing what a difference one little truth can make in a person's life? When you know the truth, the truth will indeed set you free.

Scriptures about Helplessness and Powerlessness

Of course there are many Scriptures that assure us that there is nothing too difficult for God. It is good to read and memorize these truths so that they are available whenever we need them, but we need to learn them both intellectually and experientially. Intellectually we may know the truth, but the Lord may take us through various life situations in order to teach us experientially as well, by speaking through His Holy Spirit to us during our experiences. Consider the following Scriptures that speak about God's power.

> "Do not fear, for I am with you; do not anxiously look about you, for I am your God. I will strengthen you, surely I will help you, Surely I will uphold you with My righteous right hand." (Isaiah 41:10)

"My grace is sufficient for you, for power is perfected in weakness." (2 Corinthians 12:9)

"Most gladly, therefore, I will rather boast about my weaknesses, that the power of Christ may dwell in me." (2 Corinthians 12:9)

"I can do all things through Him who strengthens me." (Philippians 4:13)

"Have I not commanded you? Be strong and courageous! Do not tremble or be dismayed, for the Lord your God is with you wherever you go." (Joshua 1:9)

"With men it is impossible, but not with God; for all things are possible with God." (Mark 10:27)

Overcoming feelings of Helplessness

The truth is that many times we are helpless and too small to defend ourselves, but the larger truth is that the Lord is always with us to defend us and strengthen us. In times of difficulty we need to cry out to the Lord and listen to His voice. When we do this He will use His Holy Spirit to "guide [us] into all the truth," (John 16:13) and this truth will give us the "peace of God , which surpasses all comprehension," (Philippians 4:7) so that we do not feel overwhelmed by our circumstances.

The steps to freedom from feelings of helplessness are the same as those given in previous chapters. They can be summarized as follows:

1. Identify the feelings of helplessness.
2. Identify the root events underlying your feelings of helplessness.
3. Identify the root beliefs causing you to feel helpless.
4. Pray for the Lord to bring truth to you about your belief that your situation is helpless.

CHAPTER 11

Dealing with Feelings of Shame and Defilement

K aren," an elderly woman, sought counseling for feelings of depression and worthlessness. She stated that she became depressed several years after her husband died. His death did not bother her, because he was so mean to her, and she had been angry at him for how badly he had treated her over the years. Her husband drank and had many affairs, but she was glad that he had sex with other women because she felt that sex was evil and she refused to have sex with him. Karen attended church regularly and pretended to be happy, but admitted that she was a hypocrite, and eventually realized how angry she really was. Although she no longer felt angry at her husband, she felt guilty for holding in her anger for so many years and pretending to be happy and for being unkind to him. She believed that since she deliberately held her anger in and refused to forgive her husband, God would not forgive her.

I asked Karen how she usually dealt with guilt, and she indicated that she usually just ignored it. However, she stated that she knew she should confess it to the Lord. When I asked her if she would like to get rid of her guilt feelings she said that she would, so I led her in a prayer of confession for holding onto her anger for so many years and for being a hypocrite. After confessing this, however, she continued to express feelings of guilt. It was apparent that although she had confessed her sins and the Lord had forgiven her she still held onto feelings of false shame that were tormenting her.

Root Beliefs underlying False Guilt and Shame

The beliefs that are typically held by those who experience false shame are usually rooted in early-life experiences. Even though these individuals confess their sins before God, they continue to feel shameful and guilty and cannot release these negative feelings.

A pastor was referred to me who came from a denomination that placed a great deal of emphasis upon holy living. Although holy living is a good thing, this poor man lived in torment about inconsequential matters. He wanted to do what pleased God, but no matter what he did he always felt that he failed and was never able to please God. When I asked him what he felt guilty about he stated, "I have a camper that I sometimes feel that I should sell and give the money to the Lord, but I can't make up my mind. When I decide to sell it, then I feel that I am doing the wrong thing because I should use it for serving the Lord." Regardless of what he prayed, he felt certain that he could never please God, and he feared that he would lose his faith and eventually forsake God.

These feelings were obviously not based upon the truth, but even as we discussed the Scriptures this poor man was unable to appropriate them, and he continued to live in torment day and night. Such feelings are rooted in past experiences that need to be identified by asking the individual when they first felt such feelings. This will often take them to the root event where these beliefs were first developed, and then the underlying beliefs will need to be identified. The following are the most common beliefs behind such false guilt and shame.

- I am a bad, shameful person.
- It was my fault.
- I should have known better.
- I participated willingly in this behavior so I am at fault.
- Even God cannot forgive me for what I've done.

- I should have done something to stop it.
- I should have told someone.

Steps for Dealing with False Guilt and Shame

Many people suffer from false guilt and what I choose to call "shame." This is a feeling of guilt, blame, and a belief that they are bad, and deserving of more punishment than they have received, even though they have appropriate feelings of remorse and may have confessed their true guilt. Such feelings can continue to torment the individual and lead them to engage in destructive actions such as self-harm, high-risk behaviors, and masochistic behaviors, and keep them experiencing depressive emotions.

This is a very common experience for individuals who have been sexually abused as children and have developed deeply rooted beliefs that they are bad and unloveable individuals because of what they have done. No matter how much you attempt to convince them that it was not their fault because they were children and the perpetrator was an adult or a person much older than themselves, they will continue to persist in their negative feelings of shame.

Janet was a young mother of three children who was shocked to discover that her husband of fourteen years had been having numerous affairs. She had mixed feelings of anger, betrayal, hurt, and confusion but when I asked her what her strongest feeling was she said that her strongest feeling was shame. This surprised me that she would feel shame when her husband was the one who obviously should feel shame for his behavior so I asked her, "why do you feel shame?"

"Because I feel that this would not have happened if I taken better care of myself and been more responsive to his sexual desires. I think I should have fixed my hair nicer, treated him nicer, made him better meals, and been willing to do more fun things with him. He sometimes called me an 'old fuddy' because I wouldn't go out with him sometimes to party."

It was obvious that these feelings of shame were irrational and based upon some past experience but I knew better than to try to talk her out of them. "Would you be willing to try to remember the first time you felt such feelings of shame?" She nodded her approval and I prayed for her, "Lord, please take Janet to the source and origin of these feelings that it was her fault that her husband began having affairs because she did not take care of herself as well as she should have?"

Janet quickly began to cry and she stated that the first time she felt this way was when she was six years old and an uncle molested her. She explained that the uncle promised to make her something she wanted in exchange for some sexual favors. As a small child she participated in the favors and then felt deeply ashamed afterwards and she felt that it was her fault. Even though her uncle later apologized, changed his life and she forgave him, she still carried these feelings of shame deep within her heart.

While Janet was recalling this memory and feeling the shame I prayed for her, "Lord, what do you want this little girl to know about her feelings of shame and believing this was her fault?" Now just listen quietly and see if any thoughts come into your mind.

She immediately replied, "I just had one thought; I know it's not true. It wasn't my fault."

"Does that feel true to say it's not your fault?" I asked.

"Yes. I know it's true. I was too young to know better. I didn't think he would do anything to hurt me. I trusted him."

"Where do you think that thought came from?" I asked. "I know it came from the Lord" she replied because I've known it was not my fault for a long time but I still felt like it was. Now I know it was untrue and it feels untrue."

I asked Janet to try to stir up the feelings of shame again but she was unable to feel them; they were completely gone. Just the simple truth from the Lord removed her feelings of shame completely. When we returned to the subject of her feelings about her husband's infidelity, those feelings were also gone because they were based upon these earlier feelings and experiences.

This illustrates the simple process involved in releasing an individual of false guilt and shame, using the same steps identified previously. First, identify the negative feeling the person is having, which was shame in this case. Second, identify the original source or root cause of the feelings, meaning the initial event that gave root to the false guilt. Third, identify the underlying beliefs that the person holds that continue to stir up feelings of shame and false guilt. And then, fourth, ask the Lord to bring the truth to the person's mind.

Dealing with Feelings of Dirtiness and Defilement

The well-known hymn "There is a Fountain" written by William Cowper says,

> There is a fountain filled with blood drawn from Immanuel's veins;
> And sinners, plunged beneath that flood, lose all their guilty stains.
> Lose all their guilty stains, lose all their guilty stains;
> And sinners plunged beneath that flood, lose all their guilty stains.

There is a wonderful truth expressed in these words, that even the deepest stains that we have in our lives can be cleansed by the blood and forgiveness of the Lord Jesus. Some feelings of guilt go way beyond the normal feelings of guilt that we all have, and some people feel that that are so deeply stained by having been involved in certain activities that they can never be cleansed. They feel that they have been so intrinsically and permanently stained, tainted, and defiled that others can see their defilement and want nothing to do with them, and not even God can stand to be around them.

This is very common with individuals who have been sexually abused. They often are shamed by family members who blame them for the abuse, so they are unable to talk about the abuse, and feel that they are forever stained by the abuse events. The Scriptures speak to us of such stains in several passages that reassure us that no matter how deep the stains may be, we can be cleansed from all of them through the blood of the Lamb of God.

> Purify me with hyssop, and I shall be clean; Wash me, and I shall be whiter than snow. Psalm 51:7

> "Come now, and let us reason together," Says the Lord. Though your sins are as scarlet, They will be as white as snow; Though they are red like crimson, They will be like wool. Isaiah 1:18

> If we confess our sins, He is faithful and righteous to forgive us our sins and to cleanse us from all unrighteousness. 1 John 1:9

> These are the ones who come out of the great tribulation, and they have washed their robes and made them white in the blood of the Lamb. Revelation 7:14

Notice especially the words of the apostle John in 1 John 1:9 which tell us that our confession of our sins not only results in forgiveness but a cleansing "from all unrighteousness." The Lord not only wants us to know that we are forgiven but that we are completely cleansed from all stains in our lives. Once we are forgiven and cleansed then the Lord looks upon us and sees His own holy Son. Once we are cleansed by the blood of Jesus we become clothed in the "righteousness of Christ." Isaiah 61:10 says, "He has clothed me with garments of salvation, He has wrapped me with a robe of righteousness, As a bridegroom decks himself with a garland, And as a bride adorns herself with her jewels."

Root Beliefs Underlying Feelings of Defilement

Feelings of dirtiness that remain after confession of sins are caused, once again, by deep-rooted beliefs from earlier experiences that implanted the following beliefs.

- I am so tainted and stained by what I've done that I can never be cleansed.

- Not even God can stand to see me.
- This can never be removed from me.
- I'm dirty and defiled because of what happened to me.
- Everyone can tell that I'm dirty.
- I'll never be clean again.
- No one will ever be able to love me after what I've done.
- My body is dirty.
- I will never be happy again.

"Marcia" was in her fourth marriage and felt stressed because her elderly father, whom she cared for, was emotionally abusive to her husband, but she was too fearful to speak with him about his behavior and to risk upsetting him. When I asked her to try to remember the first time she felt this way, she stated that it was when she was six years old and her uncle had molested her. When she reported this to her parents they both blamed her and were angry at her. She remembered the angry scowl on her father's face and feeling very shameful and dirty. I asked her permission to pray for her.

"Lord," I prayed. "What do you want this little girl to know about her feelings that she was dirty and shameful because of what happened to her?"

Marcia began to cry, and I asked her to share what thoughts were coming to her mind. "I was never really alone; the Lord was with me. I have people with me now, too. My husband is with me. It wasn't my fault. I'm not a bad, shameful person. I'm okay."

I asked Marcia if those thoughts felt true, and she indicated that they did. After she finished sharing the thoughts in her mind, I asked her to think about that incident and tell me how she felt. She stated that she felt much better. On a 10-point scale she rated her feelings of shame and defilement as a "1," in contrast to her feelings before we prayed, which she had rated as a "15" on a 10-point scale. The Lord gave her peace as He brought the truth into her mind in that memory. A number of other emotional and behavioral changes also resulted from that session including a new freedom to confront her stepfather about his verbally abusive behavior toward her husband.

Steps to Release from Feeling Defiled

The steps to being released from these feelings are the same as those discussed in dealing with feelings of shame. These steps are as follows.

1. Identify the negative feeling you are having, which was shame in this case.
2. Identify the original event or root cause of the feelings, meaning the initial event that gave root to the false guilt.
3. Identify the underlying beliefs that you hold that continue to stir up feelings of shame and false guilt.
4. Ask the Lord to bring the truth to your mind.

CHAPTER 12

Dealing with Feelings of Hurt and Rejection

J ane" reported feeling very irritated and impatient recently with people who wasted her time, and she felt that this was related somehow to her childhood. She became impatient with her husband when it took him a long time to place an order with a company, and she became very irritated with their pastor who was providing them some financial counseling. Although he was pleasant and gracious, he spent a lot of time talking without doing any counseling, and she wanted him to get to the point and not waste her time.

I asked Jane to try to remember the first time she felt this way and she began talking about her experiences as a teenager. She was raised in a very strict home and was sent to a private Christian school as a child. As a teenager she had arthritis that made it difficult for her to walk normally and sometimes wore braces. She also took medication that clouded her thinking and made it difficult for her to study and think clearly in school. She lived in fear much of the time in school that she would be late to her next class, and sometimes ran between classes to make sure she wasn't late. In spite of her best efforts, she was late at times and had to spend much time waiting in a disciplinary line. Whenever it was her turn to be seen for discipline she had to walk in front of hundreds students and she was very embarrassed to do this.

In the 7th grade Jane was often teased often by her peers. They snickered at her and ridiculed her because her father

made her wear ill-fitting, unfashionable clothing to school.
She felt very embarrassed and hurt by these peers and felt she
was unwanted and rejected by them. I asked her if I could pray
for her about that experience and she gave her permission. I
prayed, "Lord, what is it that you want this young lady to know
right now?"

With her eyes closed, Jane listened to the Lord in prayer.
"Now I'm not ridiculed. It's over."

"Okay." "Is there anything else that comes to you?" I
asked.

"Those who ridiculed me then, are messed up now. They
were just in pain as children. Some of them were abused," Jane
replied.

"All right," I said. "Lord, is there anything else that you
want Jane to know right now?"

"I know that I'm okay now. I look okay and no one makes
fun of me anymore. It's all over."

"Thank you, Lord, for those truths," I prayed.

After this brief time of prayer Jane no longer felt hurt by
her peers. We also prayed about her feelings of anxiety about
wasting time and she received healing truths that set her free
from feeling so irritated with others who wasted her time.
Those memories no longer bothered her and she was no longer
triggered by them. Healing for such memories can go a long
way toward helping an individual get along with their wife or
husband without becoming so easily hurt.

The Example of the Lord Jesus
As discussed in Chapter 3, some feelings of anger are fact-
based or truth-based, because even the Lord Jesus became angry
when He saw evil occurring. But He never felt anger that was
based upon feelings of hurt and rejection, even though He was
rejected by the religious leaders and constantly challenged by
them. In John 2:24-25 the Scriptures tell us that "Jesus, on His
part, was not entrusting Himself to them, for He knew all men,
and because He did not need anyone to bear witness concerning
man for He Himself knew what was in man." This is the reason

why Jesus did not become angry like we do when we are rejected
or challenged by others; He "knew all men" and "knew what was
in man." In other words, Jesus understood the truth about men,
and He knew the underlying reasons and motivations of their
hearts and did not need their affirmation in any way.

In contrast, the rest of humanity is constantly looking
for affirmation that they are okay, they are accepted, and they
are wanted. Jesus did not have these emotional needs because
He had all truth within Him and the truth set Him free from
these emotional struggles. The underlying lies we believe about
ourselves are what most often trigger off angry reactions, and
He did not have any of these lies. The angry reactions of others
lead us to overreact to them at times and are the source of many
church splits and relationship problems between Christians.

Nowhere can we see the fallibility of Christians more
clearly than in the politics and relationships of churches. Most
church conflicts have nothing to do with doctrinal differences,
but have everything to do with hurt feelings when people feel
overlooked, unappreciated, or slighted by someone else.

Paul spent a great deal of time in his epistles addressing
such problems within the early New Testament churches, and
many of them had to do with personal relationship problems.
This is why Paul exhorted the Philippian church in Philippians
2:1-8 to have the "attitude in yourselves which was also in Christ
Jesus." A humble, servant's attitude can protect us from being
offended and reacting to our Christian brothers and sisters
with jealousy or hurt. If we cannot overcome our hurt through
prayer and simple obedience to these Scriptures, then we need
to seek direction and truth from the Lord so that we can uproot
the beliefs and feelings that cause us to repeatedly overreact to
others around us. These same feelings will cause individuals to
overreact to their spouses and create serious marital problems,
if they are not dealt with quickly.

Feelings of Hurt and Rejection
One of the most common emotions that we feel when we
are mistreated by others is the feeling of hurt. This sometimes

comes through simple events in our lives, such as a parent angrily telling a child to go away when they are trying to work and the child wants to play, or it can occur through verbal abuse. The child interprets the event in either case as proof that he is not important and he is unloved, and this becomes a major lie that leads him to being over-sensitive and to overreacting any time someone is untactful or slightly critical of him. Sometimes these feelings originate in relatively harmless events in a child's life, and sometimes they result from years of emotional and mental abuse that become a theme of their life. Either way the underlying lies are the same, and the truth is needed in those memories to set the individual free.

A young lady left home to escape her over-controlling father and a few years later settled down, got married, and wanted to reconnect with her dad. However, he was hurt by her departure and he remained distant and cold toward her, and she felt very hurt and missed him very much. She made a trip back home and spent time with her paternal aunt and paternal grandmother, but her father made no effort to come see her, and she was deeply hurt again. The prayer minister prayed for the Lord to take her back to the source and origin of her feelings of hurt, and she stated that when she was young it was a pervasive, everyday experience that her father was angry at her, she could not please him no matter how hard she tried, and she felt that she was a burden to him. She believed that she was unwanted and in the way, and was afraid to call him on the phone for fear that he would be angry and rejecting toward her.

After identifying the emotion of hurt, identifying the source of these feelings, and identifying these lies, the minister prayed for the Lord to bring her truth about these beliefs. She immediately had the thought that her father was just speaking out of anger, she sometimes does the same with her husband when she is angry, and she remembered that sometimes her father had told her that she was the best thing that ever happened to him. She teared up with joy at this memory of times when her father told her that he could not have lived without her. After receiving these truths she stated that she no longer felt hurt and she had no more fear of calling her father. She called her father the next day and had a wonderful talk with him, and he told her how proud he was of how she had grown up.

Hurt feelings are often disguised as feelings of anger because many people prefer to hide their personal feelings of hurt, but they are less embarrassed to show their anger. In a previous chapter we talked about justifiable anger as anger that is caused by serious harms committed against a person, such as physical abuse and literal abandonment. Even the Lord Jesus was justifiably angry at times when He observed the hardness of heart of His enemies or the evil of men. Sometimes we become angry at such evil also, but much of the anger manifested by men is unjustifiable and results from misinterpretations and from feeling hurt or rejected by others.

I remember an incident as a child when I was in the seventh grade and was asked to stand in front of my class and read a story. I was very shy and soft-spoken, and when I began reading the teacher told me to read louder. I started over and began reading louder but it was not loud enough so she told me to read louder still. I began reading louder but I was still too quiet so she said a third time, "Louder." I began to feel embarrassed standing in front of my peers and felt like I was being "dressed down" in front of everyone. Finally, I became angry and began reading in what felt like a shout. The teacher finally said "Good. That's just about right." I finished the reading assignment "shouting" each word out and then sat down feeling very angry, but the underlying feeling behind the anger was a feeling of hurt and embarrassment.

Long into my adult years I found myself becoming irritated and angry at others who could not hear me or understand me. When I spoke to someone who was hard of hearing or was not a native English speaker and I had to repeat myself several times it irritated me. Or when others leaned toward me and cocked their heads to hear me because I spoke so softly it triggered off feelings of embarrassment and anger, even though I knew that I was soft-spoken. This was not a justifiable anger but rather an anger triggered by underlying feelings of embarrassment that originated in a childhood experience. The solution to it was finding truth from the Lord to replace the lies and misinterpretations that I carried with me all those years. And I know that you have similar things in your life that trigger you off also.

Root Beliefs Underlying Feelings of Hurt

Some of the lies that people believe when they feel hurt are:

- I am unimportant
- I am not wanted, loved, or valued
- My feelings are not important
- I am worthless
- No one cares for me
- I cannot measure up no matter how hard I try
- I am unacceptable
- I cannot please others because _____
- I was a burden
- I am in the way; I am not liked,
- I am not appreciated
- I am not affirmed or validated
- My feelings are not important

Biblical Examples of Hurt Feelings

In Genesis 4 we read the account of Cain and Abel, the first two children of Adam and Eve. From the biblical accounts there is no reason for us to believe that either of them had been abused. They were both probably loved equally by their parents and neither of them had been ridiculed or rejected by their peers since they had none. However, one day they both brought an offering to the Lord and the Lord "had regard for Abel and for his offering" (Genesis 4:4) but not for Cain's offering. We are told in verse 5 that "Cain became very angry and his countenance fell." Apparently, he felt hurt and rejected by the Lord even though the Lord clearly did not reject his offering in a hurtful way.

The Lord said to Cain in verses 6 and 7, "Why are you angry? And why has your countenance fallen? If you do well, will not your countenance be lifted up? And if you do not do well, sin is crouching at the door; and its desire is for you, but you must master it." The Lord told Cain that if he did well (probably meaning that he should also offer a blood offering as Abel had) that his offering would also be "accepted" (See KJV). All he had to do was approach the Lord with a sacrificial offering that represented the blood offering of the coming Messiah rather than an offering of crops that represented his good works. But Cain would not do as the Lord instructed him, and he chose to interpret the Lord's request in a negative way and refused to let go of his angry feelings. The Lord warned him that this would result in sin and that sin was "crouching at the door" but he held onto his negative feelings. In the following verse we are told that when Cain was in the field with Abel he rose up against him and killed him, due to his anger.

Cain's angry feelings were actually feelings of hurt that he nursed and harbored until he eventually killed his own brother who was an innocent victim who had done no wrong to Cain. That's the way that sin often occurs; it begins with a feeling that festers for awhile and eventually erupts into a sinful act that damages innocent bystanders. That is why the apostle Paul warns us in Ephesians 4:26, "Be angry, and yet do not sin; do not let the sun go down on your anger." Feelings of hurt often result in extreme anger and violence.

Another example of such hurt-based anger can be found in 2 Samuel 10 when king Nahash died and his son Hanun became the king of the Ammonites. David sent some of his servants to console the new king in honor of his father, but Hanun was misguided by some of his advisors and misinterpreted the kindness of David as a covert attempt to spy on them. In anger he humiliated David's servants by shaving off half of their beards and cutting off their garments in the middle. When David learned of this he was righteously angry at Hanun's actions and he instructed his men to remain at Jericho until their beards had grown back, but he did not send out his army to fight them until the Ammonites, realizing their mistake, feared that Israel would attack them so they hired the Syrians and gathered their army together against Israel. When David saw that the Ammonites and the Syrians were preparing to attack the Israelites, he sent out his army and they battled with them and defeated them all. After the Syrians were thoroughly defeated they made peace with the Israelites. All of this, however, was the result of Hanun's misinterpretations of David's action and feeling hurt and angry at him.

Marital Counseling and feelings of Hurt

The majority of man's anger, I believe, is lie-based, rather than truth-based anger, and it is seen often in relationship problems. Many people are very sensitive to the words or actions of their family members and friends because they have been hurt previously, and they continue to hold onto the internal lies that were sown from the past hurts. They will remain in bondage to these past experiences and lies until the Lord brings healing to their minds in those places. What happens in many marital and relationship problems is that one party becomes hurt by a comment or action of a second party due to unresolved feelings of hurt, and when the injured person reacts back it triggers off the hurt feelings of the first person. This sets off an escalating chain reaction between the two people. However, when one of the individuals receives truth and some emotional healing about his past hurts, it breaks the chain and the two individuals are then free to move out of the conflict.

Marital counseling is an especially difficult and challenging undertaking and most counselors find it very frustrating and unproductive. During my thirty years as a counselor I used a variety of marital counseling approaches as a mental health counselor and most of the time felt ineffective and hopeless about it. However, since I have begun focusing upon the individual hurt feelings and unresolved emotional issues of the spouses and begun praying with them for truth, I have experienced great success in working with couples. I have come to the conclusion that most marital problems are the result of unresolved past issues that are triggered off by the actions or words of one member of the couple, and that these problems will continue to occur until at least one of them receives healing. It helps tremendously for the two of them to accept the basic principle that their spouse is not the cause of their upset feelings; rather their internal beliefs are what cause their feelings. This insight opens up dialogue sometimes, but will not bring improvement in the relationship until at least one of the spouses receives some truth into his or her mind so that they quit reacting with so much hurt and anger.

Steps for Overcoming feelings of Hurt

The truth is that everyone has been hurt and rejected at some time in their life. We all can recall times as children when someone did not like us or someone teased us or picked on us. The result is that we are still sensitive to what other people say about us or the way they treat us. It is a rare person, indeed, who never becomes upset when someone insults them or dislikes them. Even mature Christians can be offended and hurt because they have some roots of rejection that become triggered and reawakened at times. We need to seek to become like the Lord Jesus who "knew all men" and "knew what was in man" so that He did not entrust Himself to them. The way that we have our minds renewed so that we can become more like the Lord in this matter is to notice when we are feeling hurt or insecure and then turn to the Lord for emotional healing.

The steps to freedom from feelings of hurt are the same as those given in previous chapters for dealing with other belief-based feelings. They can be summarized as follows:

1. Identify your feelings of hurt.
2. Identify the root events underlying your feelings of hurt.
3. Identify the root beliefs causing you to feel hurt.
4. Pray for the Lord to bring truth to you about your belief that you are worthless, unwanted, or unacceptable.

SECTION C

PROCESSES AND PRINCIPLES

CHAPTER 13

Hindrances to Emotional Healing Prayer

When I first learned these basic prayer principles I was elated to see how God was able to release individuals from deeply held beliefs that had held them in bondage. It wasn't long, however, before I began to encounter some difficulties. The first time was with a gentleman who had been sexually abused as a child and had developed some severe emotional and behavioral difficulties. During my first session with him everything went well. I identified the painful emotion he was experiencing, we quickly traced it to its origin and identified the underlying lies he had learned, and then I prayed and the Lord brought truth to his mind.

Both of us were eager to continue with this process, but when we met a second time and identified the next underlying lie and prayed for truth, nothing happened. I prayed again, and still nothing happened so I prayed a third time and nothing happened. I was stunned and embarrassed, and this gentleman was just as disappointed. After this session I went back to some of the sources where I had learned these prayer principles and began looking for explanations. What was wrong? What had I missed? Why did the Lord show up the first time to bring truth but not the second time? Over time I began to realize that there were five major reasons why a person may not receive emotional healing when they pray for truth.

Harboring Anger and Resentment

The first reason that the Lord may not respond to our prayer when we ask Him for His truth is that we may have some anger that is hindering us from hearing from the Lord. Whether it is justified anger or belief-based anger, it can interfere with the healing process and prevent the Lord from responding to our prayer. Although I never had the opportunity to attempt further prayer with the man mentioned above, it is very likely that he had unresolved feelings of resentment that were interfering with our prayers. This certainly fits with the Scriptures that tell us, "your iniquities have made a separation between you and your God, And your sins have hidden His face from you, so that He does not hear" (Isaiah 59:2). Jesus himself told us in the Sermon on the Mount, "if you forgive men for their transgressions, your heavenly Father will also forgive you. But if you do not forgive men, then your Father will not forgive your transgressions" (Matthew 6:14-15). The clear implication here is that the Lord will not listen to our prayers when we harbor unforgiveness in our hearts. If you pray for the Lord to bring you, or someone else, truth and nothing happens it may be because they need to first deal with some anger they are harboring.

I was praying with a sixteen-year-old girl once who had been deeply hurt and offended by her father whom she felt had abandoned her. The primary emotion that she expressed seemed to be feelings of hurt, so I traced these to the original source and identified the underlying lie she was believing and prayed for the Lord to bring her truth. Nothing happened, so I prayed again and still nothing happened. I began to feel a little panicky, because the youth pastor of her church and her mother were both present and I wanted them to witness the Lord's healing, but it was not working. I began to wonder what was blocking the process and finally questioned her about her anger. She admitted that she was very angry at her father and didn't know if she could ever forgive him. I asked her what would happen if she was to forgive him (to identify the lie that was preventing her from moving forward) and she stated that he would get away with his selfish behavior and she felt his wrongs were so great that it was her responsibility to hold him accountable by remaining angry at him. With this belief exposed I asked her if she would be willing to listen to the Lord address this belief, and she said she would.

I then prayed and she began to cry. I inquired as to what thoughts came into her mind and she stated, "It's not my job to punish my dad. The Lord said that was His job and only He could punish him correctly." I asked her if she still wanted to hold onto her anger and she said she did not, so I led her in a prayer to release her justified anger toward her father. Then I asked the young lady how she felt about her father now and she stated that she was no longer angry at him, but she just missed him and the closeness they had had previously. In some cases, the individual has such strong anger that it needs to become the first focus of attention before turning to other emotional issues. After removing this young lady's anger we then were able to focus on her feelings of sadness and grief at having lost the closeness that she once had with her father. I never saw this young lady again, but her youth pastor reported that she was doing much better and was no longer angry at her father.

Unwilling to Face the Pain Due to Protective Beliefs

This example illustrates another major reason why some individuals will not hear from the Lord when they pray for truth. They may be unwilling to relinquish their negative feelings or to hear from the Lord due to protective lies they hold. Protective lies are beliefs that stand out front in the person's mind and prevent them from moving forward into their memories or being willing to hear the truth. All of us have some protective lies that prevent us from accessing the source of our emotional pain, or from being willing to hear the truth from the Lord. When an individual is unable to remember the source of their emotional pain, it is usually due to their unwillingness to re-experience the pain.

When this occurs, simply ask the prayer recipient if he/she would be "willing" to remember the source or to "hear" what the Lord wants them to know. If they are willing, then go ahead and pray for them and ask the Lord what He wants them to know about their belief. The Lord will bring them the truth they need, if they are truly willing to hear from Him, and then you can move on in the ministry session. If they are unwilling to remember the source or "hear" what the Lord wants them to know, you can sometimes ask "why?" and pray about the belief that is impeding them. However, there are times when their unwillingness will prevent any further ministry progress until a future date when they become willing again.

Sharon had been verbally abused by her stepfather as a child prayed about some early memories and received some healing for her feelings of hurt. She received some truth and then indicated that she felt better but she still felt some negative feelings. When the counselor questioned her about these negative feelings she eventually identified them as anger toward her father for being so critical of her, for teaching her that women are inferior, and for showing favoritism toward her brother. The counselor affirmed her right to her anger but asked her how long she wanted to hold onto her anger and she replied that she was not ready to release it yet.

The counselor, recognizing that this was a "protective lie" asked her what would happen if she were to release this anger and she stated that she would no longer have an excuse for her failures. She also believed that she needed her anger to protect her from her stepfather's continuing verbal abuse. The counselor then asked her if she would be willing to know what the Lord wanted her to know about this and she said that she was so he prayed, "Lord, what do you want Sharon to know about this belief that she needs to hand onto her anger in order to protect herself from her stepfather and to have an excuse for her failures. Sharon began crying and stated, "He said that He would protect me and that I don't need any excuses for my failures." Once the Lord removed her lies she was then ready to give up her feelings of anger and to pray for the Lord to carry them for her.

Focusing on the Wrong Feelings

A third hindrance to hearing from the Lord is when you are focused on the wrong feelings and the wrong beliefs. For example, in the chapter on grief I mentioned a woman I prayed with who was struggling with feelings about her husband having left her for another woman. For several sessions I thought she was feeling rejected and hurt by her husband and I prayed repeatedly for the Lord to bring her truth and nothing happened. Finally, I reconsidered her feelings and asked if she felt grief. She immediately responded, "Yes, yes, that's what I feel. I feel all this grief and sorrow that he is gone." We then prayed about her grief and asked the Lord to carry it for her and to remove it from her, and she immediately felt relief as the Lord lifted those feelings and carried them for her.

Each emotion has different underlying beliefs and if you are focusing on the wrong emotions, you will be praying for truth in an area that does not need correction. Nothing happens when you pray about the wrong feelings and beliefs. This requires much discernment on the part of the prayer minister, because if you do not understand the individual's true feelings then you will be unable to pray for the specific beliefs he/she is believing.

Losing Touch with Feelings

The fourth hindrance to healing truths is when individuals lose touch with their feelings during the prayer session. Prayer is most effective in releasing the individual when they strongly feel the emotions and are not trying to suppress them. We all have suppressed our feelings at times because we did not know anything else to do with them. This enables us to function in life, so that we can continue performing our jobs and basic life responsibilities in spite of unresolved emotions. But when we are ready to obtain healing and release from these emotions, we need to be honest with ourselves and with God and allow our feelings to be experienced and expressed. Once we allow ourselves to feel our emotions completely then we can do as David often did when he "cried to the Lord," (Psalm 120:1) so that the Lord can answer us and comfort us with His truth. Psalm 34:17-18 says, "The righteous cry and the Lord hears, And delivers them out of all their troubles. The Lord is near to the brokenhearted, And saves those who are crushed in spirit."

Some individuals have suppressed so many feelings for so long that they hold tightly onto their emotions and are afraid to let them out, but in order to receive healing they must choose to slowly release them. Those who have been deeply abused need to have a mature, experienced prayer minister to assist them and should have a strong Christian counselor available to help as well. These helpers must be very sensitive to the readiness of the individual and not push them into disclosing any feelings or memories until they are fully ready. Seriously traumatized and abused individuals can be flooded with such powerful emotions and memories that the minister may be unable to bring full resolution and leave them feeling emotionally vulnerable after the session ends. In such cases it is essential that they seek help from a profession Christian counselor who has experience with such severe cases of abuse.

God works in the realm of truth and reality, and when we suppress our emotions and rationalize our feelings we are not being honest with Him about our feelings and our true beliefs. While individuals are praying for emotional healing they need to be encouraged frequently to let themselves feel their feelings and make no attempts to suppress them. If they lose touch with their feelings during the session, the prayer minister should simply back up to a point where the recipient can begin feeling the emotions strongly again. Encourage them to remain in contact with their emotions until they have a chance to identify the lies and pray for the truth. It is when they are being completely honest with the Lord and "in touch" with their true emotions that the Lord is able to bring them the maximum comfort through His truth.

Many people have layers upon layers of emotions that make it difficult for them to sort them out. You may be like a ball of yarn with each strand representing a different emotion, and your task is to unravel this ball one strand at a time, beginning with the biggest one and working on down systematically to the smaller ones. The stronger the emotion, however, the better the result will be when you pray, so it is important to select the most prominent emotion to focus on initially. As one emotion is resolved then you can move to the next one, until you are ready to quit or until your available time is used up.

Failing to Identify the Original Source

The fifth major hindrance to receiving truth from the Lord is when you have not identified the original source of your feelings. Many adults have difficulty connecting their present feelings to the past, but when they have strong belief-based emotions from present experiences there are always early experiences that are exacerbating their present reactions. The exception, of course, is when the individual is experiencing fact-based emotions such as justified anger, grief, guilt, sadness, and disappointment. Other than these exceptions, strong emotional feelings have earlier sources that need to be identified.

In order to identify the earlier sources, it helps to focus on present feelings and then try to remember the first time you experienced a similar feeling. Sometimes, individuals purposely have suppressed these memories and cannot remember them, and it may help to confirm to the Lord that you are indeed willing to remember any earlier memories that may be connected to the present emotions. It often helps to ask the Lord to take you to the source and origin of your present feelings.

One middle-aged man was praying about his feelings about his wife who was involved with another man, and he could not connect his feelings to any earlier memories. After repeated attempts he still could not remember an earlier time when he had felt this way so I asked him if he was willing to remember any earlier times when he felt similarly. He affirmed that he was willing, so I then prayed "Lord, please take 'Bob' to the source of these feelings where he first felt the way he does now." Immediately, he remembered an incident as a child when his father taunted him and mistreated him. We prayed about these feelings and the underlying beliefs he developed at that time, and the Lord brought truth to his mind and released him from the lies that were controlling him. This truth also released him from his fear of confronting his wife about her inappropriate behavior.

In summary, the following are the five primary hindrances to receiving truth from the Lord when we apply the prayer principles described in this book:

1.　Anger and Resentment
2.　Unwillingness due to Protective Beliefs
3.　Focus on wrong feelings
4.　Losing touch with feelings
5.　Failure to identify the original source

Do not become discouraged if you follow the principles suggested in this book and nothing happens at times. It simply means that one of these five factors is interfering with the process.

CHAPTER 14

Christian Discipleship and Counseling

It is important that the reader understand that not all human problems result from misinterpretations and not all negative emotions can be resolved through this prayer process. Many times there are underlying emotional factors that contribute heavily to personality and character flaws and as you pray with individuals and see them being released from their core lies and beliefs they will experience profound changes in their behaviors. But there are a number of other factors that may contribute heavily to an individual's personal struggles. Sometimes it is necessary for individuals to receive some discipleship instruction in practical matters or to be assisted by caring, mature Christians to make some deliberate changes in their life based upon biblical principles. The following are some examples of discipleship topics that may need to be addressed with specific individuals.

Discipleship Topics
Immaturity and Irresponsibility

Dealing with negative emotions can free a person from feelings of anxiety, anger or depression and can change their behaviors in many ways. However, it will not make an immature person become suddenly mature. If you have been an irresponsible, lazy, and self-centered person before receiving healing prayer you will probably continue to be so after receiving emotional healing. It will require you to make a deliberate choice to behave in a responsible manner and may even require the admonition of the Scriptures and of mature Christian friends to motivate you to begin behaving in a mature manner.

Some individuals who were overprotected and overindulged as children and have become dependent upon others, as an adult, to provide for them. Even when their parents pass away, the government sometimes supports them as disabled persons or provides welfare checks for them when they are capable of working and are not truly disabled. When this happens they become dependent upon government handouts and may never achieve independence and become fully responsible. They may need to be confronted with the biblical principle that is taught extensively in the book of Proverbs and is succinctly stated for us by the apostle Paul in 2 Thessalonians 3:10, "if anyone will not work, neither let him eat." With such confrontation by a united effort of those in the person's support network the individual may eventually assume full responsibility for their own life.

Poor Relationship Skills

Some people have poor social skills and verbal skills and will continue to have weak skills in these areas after receiving emotional healing. However, if there were emotional factors that have prevented them from engaging in relationships, such as fear of rejection or an excessive fear of being alone, that have led them to be overly demanding of others and inappropriate, emotional healing may enable them to begin initiating more conversations with others or to back off from being so clingy and demanding so that they can begin to develop better skills. They can still benefit from prayer to facilitate mind renewal, but they may also need practical instructions in how to communicate with others and how to behave in a socially appropriate manner.

Lack of Discipline

There are some individuals who suffer problems as a result of their disorganization and lack of discipline. One man I counseled struggled with financial problems and became so deeply indebted that he became suicidal. He held a good job that provided adequate income, but habitually lived above his means and did not discipline himself to live within his budget. When he was able to find low income housing for himself and his family, his depression suddenly lifted and he began spending wildly on new appliances and new furniture rather than using his new income surplus to begin paying off his debts.

It may be that someone you know has compulsive spending habits due to lies they believe and due to spending money as a way of dealing with their negative feelings. If such is the case, try to discern the underlying feelings and beliefs that surface just prior to going on a spending spree. But if they have been accustomed to having everything they wanted and will not discipline themselves to live within their means, they may need instructions in biblical financial principles and some exhortations from a mature Christian friend to learn how to develop discipline. If their friends and acquaintances choose to withhold funds from them based upon the principle in 2 Thessalonians 3:10 they will eventually learn to live within their means, but if organizations and the society around them continue to provide them their basic necessities without any accountability or responsibility they may never learn to behave responsibly.

Negative Attitudes

Many Christian teachers and ministers teach the importance of positive thinking and encourage believers to "count their blessings" just as David instructed us in Psalm 103:2- "Bless the Lord, O my soul, And forget none of His benefits." There is a need for all of us to learn to be more thankful and to focus on what we have instead of what we do not have. David also frequently exhorted us to "Praise the Lord," and this is part of God's formula for happy living. We need to cultivate the habit of praising God for His goodness and being thankful for all that we are given. At times we are all prone to become discontent and unhappy because we compare ourselves with others. There is a need for us to be reminded and exhorted to maintain a positive attitude, and to trust God when life becomes difficult.

Aimlessness

Some believers have many blessings, a satisfying marriage, a healthy family, and a reasonable income, but they have no higher purpose in their lives. When they reach midlife or later, they may become aimless and lack purpose in their lives unless they seek God's will in their life. They may experience some existential need for purpose and some emotional depression that is based upon a lack of eternal purpose. Praying alone is not going to remove these feelings. They need to seek God's purpose for their life and seek to center their life around their God-given purposes before they will find fulfillment and complete satisfaction in their life.

Isolation from Others

All people have an innate need for connectedness and involvement with others, and those who have failed to make good connections with others may experience feelings of isolation and loneliness. Many feelings of aloneness are belief-based and can be removed through healing prayer, such as the feelings of single adults and those who feel a strong need for a companion. Through prayer they can come to realize that they do not need to be married or have a life partner in order to be happy and fulfilled.

The Lord can give them a strong sense of His presence and fill their need for belonging in a miraculous way. Sometimes this can even free them so that they can more easily find a partner, because they are happier and not searching so frantically, which is much more attractive to others. However, it is clear from the Scriptures that single people can have very fulfilling lives, because the Lord Jesus was never married and yet He had a fulfilling life. The apostle Paul was unmarried and yet he had many friends and close relationships and an exciting ministry that provided him a strong sense of fulfillment. He was alone at times but was deeply involved in fellowship with other believers. Fellowship and friendship with others should be encouraged in those who are lacking them.

Failure to Serve God

Some individuals have virtually excluded God from their lives and have centered their lives around themselves and their own personal goals and material desires. Author, pastor, and sociologist Alan Jamieson in his book *A Churchless Faith (2003, SPCK, London)* states that there are many Christians today who have left the church and are attempting to live their faith on their own. He calls them "post-congregational Christians," and from his research he has found that of these Christians, ninety-four percent had been church leaders—deacons, elders, and Sunday School teachers. Thirty-two percent had been full-time ministers previously. David Barrett, author of the *World Christian Encyclopedia* (New York: Oxford University Press, 2001), estimates there are about 112 million "churchless Christians" worldwide. Many firm believers have abandoned the church because they cannot find one that satisfies their needs or they feel that it is irrelevant to their personal struggles.

Although there are no perfect churches, the Scriptures make it clear that we were created to have fellowship with God and with one another, and we are warned in Hebrews 10:25 of "not forsaking our own assemblying together, as is the habit of some." Many believers come from non-Christian homes and must find their closest relationships with other believers in their church, so it is important to find a church that is mostly in agreement with your beliefs and commit yourself to it. As you fully commit yourself to a church and become involved in every aspect of that church, you will find some much-needed fellowship with some of the other members. Those who attempt to walk on their own are likely to walk a lonely road. The Lord can take away feelings of aloneness and loneliness that are lie-based, but He never intended for us to live our lives in isolation from fellow believers and we cannot find full contentment without centering our lives around His people and His purposes. Attending a Bible-believing church can also give you a place of ministry and service for God, and give you purpose and an outlet for your abilities in serving Him.

Missing God's Will

Sometimes individuals need instruction in how to discern God's will. Whether it is in discerning God's will in finding a life partner, in pursing a vocation, or in financial matters, there are times when we all need to understand basic biblical principles for knowing the will of God in our life. We may experience feelings of confusion or anxiety due to an uncertainty about God's will for us, and prayer about these feelings might lead to some clear answers. On the other hand, people sometimes just need to have someone explain to them how to discern the will of God so that they can make a decision about what to do in a situation. Some of the principles that may be included in this process are as follows:

1.   Search the Scriptures for principles applicable to your decision.
2.   Pray for the Lord to give wisdom and direction.
3.   Seek advice from your parents and godly friends.
4.   Seek to suspend your own will so that you can discern God's promptings.
5.   After praying and developing a sense of peace about your direction, pray a few more days and then move forward if you are still at peace with this decision.

Trusting God

In Matthew 6:25, 33 in the Sermon on the Mount Jesus instructed us, "Do not be anxious for your life, as to what you shall eat, or what you shall drink; nor for your body, as to what you shall put on....But seek first His kingdom and His righteousness; and all these things shall be added to you." He called us "men of little faith" (v. 30) for worrying about these things. The truth is that we all worry about these things at times, especially when we lose a job or our income is falling short of our expenses and we're becoming more and more deeply indebted. Some of our fears and anxieties can be overcome by simply standing firm on the promises of God. We need to encourage one another and remind each other of the faithfulness of God when we are facing difficulties. And we need to remind ourselves of God's faithfulness to us in past times. However, if the anxieties continue in spite of our prayers, attempts to trust God, and meditations, then we may have deeply rooted insecurities and fears that need healing prayer.

Dealing with Behavioral Problems and Sin

The Scriptures are full of admonitions about how believers should conduct themselves in the world. They are instructed to behave in a godly way, to serve one another, and to avoid immoral activities, idolatry, strife, drunkenness, and outbursts of anger. In Galatians 5:22 the apostle Paul listed nine fruits of the Spirit that will result when we allow the Holy Spirit to control our lives. The first three of the fruits listed, love, joy, and peace, are emotions that result from allowing the Holy Spirit to remove the lies we carry within us that keep us in bondage. The remaining six fruits are behavioral characteristics that will result from having love, joy, and peace in our hearts.

Some behaviors can be stopped by choice as we come to understand the Scriptures and choose to live by their guidelines. Other behaviors are compulsive in nature and are more difficult to stop, and when this is the case it is usually because these behaviors are pain-managing behaviors that we engage in because they temporarily enable us to feel better and to escape the negative emotions we have in our lives. Prayerfully consider how your behaviors are used as a means of managing your negative emotions. As you explore your feelings just prior to engaging in these behaviors it may expose the underlying beliefs you have, and then you should pray for the Holy Spirit to replace your false beliefs with truth so that you can become freed from these behaviors.

A prayer partner can be helpful to discern how your behaviors are driven by this principle, and to discern the emotions you are experiencing just prior to engaging in the compulsive behavior, whether it is a form of substance abuse, immoral sexual impulses, aggression, violence, or other forms of compulsive behaviors. Once the preceding emotion is identified, then you need to identify the source of the emotion, identify the underlying beliefs causing the emotions, and finally pray for the Lord to bring His truth to you. When the underlying lies are removed, you will be freed from the compulsion to engage in the behavior, because you will have more peace, joy, and love in your heart in place of the pain that was there previously.

Working with Christian Counselors

Studies have shown that only 27% of surveyed psychologists identified with a Christian worldview, in contrast to the American public which is overwhelmingly religious, with almost 90% of survey respondents identifying with a religious worldview [Yarhouse, M., & Fisher, W., (2002), "Levels of training to address religion in clinical practice". *Psychotherapy: Theory/Research/Practice/Training*, 39(2), 171-176]. It would not be realistic to expect secular professional therapists to understand or be receptive to the use of Emotional Healing Prayer in helping people resolve their emotional struggles. Even those who call themselves "Christian counselors" are often skeptical and have difficulty believing in the effectiveness of prayer ministries. However, it is highly recommended that individuals work closely with a mature Christian prayer partner or a Christian counselor when you are trying to help a deeply traumatized individual or someone who is suicidal, or if you simply know that you need outside help. This is not to say that the Lord is unable to heal some people, but that He chooses to work through the members of His body, and we are limited by our own level of wisdom and discernment, and sometimes by our lack of experience and our limited training. Therefore, it is helpful to be able to communicate with professional Christian counselors about what it is that you do when you engage in this prayer process.

Probably the most prevalent counseling therapy model in use today is Cognitive Therapy. Although there are various forms of cognitive therapy, each of them shares the same basic cognitive principle that our feelings are caused primarily by the thoughts and beliefs we have, and can be changed by challenging the beliefs underlying the feelings and replacing them with more reality-centered beliefs. There are many different ways in which a person's beliefs can be challenged, but what defines cognitive therapy is not the techniques used to change the belief system of the client but the focus of the therapist on the modification of the client's belief system.

When communicating with professional counselors it may be helpful to describe this approach as a form of cognitive therapy that uses prayer to help dislodge deeply-rooted beliefs. In other words, it is "Prayer-based Cognitive Therapy." If you seek assistance from a pastor you might refer to this ministry approach as "Emotional Healing Prayer" or some similar name. The following page provides a summary of the 12 basic principles involved in "Prayer-based Cognitive Therapy" that could be useful to orient your counselor to this approach. A summary of the Basic Principles of Emotional Healing Prayer is also provided on the following page. The reader will notice that most of the principles and processes used in Emotional Healing Prayer can be described in secular terms, but the core elements given in items 4 and 8 are uniquely Christian and spiritual and are principles that a secular counselor will not understand.

As described in this book there are two basic prayer principles involved in Emotional Healing Prayer. The 1 Peter 5:7 principle is used when dealing with Type I, fact-based or truth-based emotions such as grief, sadness, disappointment, justified anger, and genuine guilt. The James 1:5 principle is used when dealing with Type II, belief-based emotions such as aloneness, false shame, defilement, fear, hurt, helplessness, hopelessness, and confusion. As you gain experience you will learn to move back and forth quickly between these two principles in finding healing. Two charts are provided at the end of this book to facilitate this process and to help you identify the underlying beliefs connected to the emotion, on which you are focusing. You are encouraged to copy these pages and hold them in front of you as you begin to practice using these two prayer principles.

Conclusion

In this chapter, we have examined some important supplementary principles for helping others find emotional freedom through Emotional Healing Prayer. The author has found that the principles outlined in this book are effective, and when healing does not occur it is because something has been overlooked. The Lord truly desires to set the captives free (Isaiah 61:1) and He wants His people to experience His peace. Even those who are unbelievers can receive healing from the Prince of Peace if they are willing to try these principles with a mature Christian. Many times it leads them to experience the reality and the goodness of the Lord, and to then open their hearts to receive Him as their personal Savior.

Much more could be written to explain how these principles can be applied to a wide range of emotional and behavioral problems that people experience, but the purpose of this book was to explain the basic prayer principles in a simple and brief way so that you can begin your healing journey or begin to help others in your ministry. If you have difficulty applying them to your own life, seek the assistance of others who have been using them effectively. It is my hope that many will find this book helpful both in their own spiritual and emotional healing and in the healing of their friends and family members. May God bless you as you begin applying these powerful principles to your life, and may you come to discover that the Lord is, indeed, the "Wonderful Counselor, the Mighty God...the Prince of Peace." As you apply these principles to your life you will discover that the Wonderful Counselor can do for you what no earthly counselor, psychologist, or doctor can do for you. He wants you to experience the truth that the "peace of God which surpasses all comprehension, shall guard your hearts and your minds in Christ Jesus" (Philippians 4:7).

Basic Principles of Prayer-based Cognitive Therapy

1.   There are two general types of emotions: belief-based emotions and fact-based emotions.

2.   Belief-based emotions are emotions that vary widely from person to person depending upon their belief system, and generally include the emotions of aloneness, shame, helplessness, hopelessness, defilement, fear, hurt, confusion, and anger.

3.   Fact-based emotions are emotions that all normal people experience when confronted with specific situations and generally include disappointment, sadness, grief, primary or justified anger, and true guilt.

4.   Fact-based emotions are best dealt with by "normalizing" them, by acknowledging the person's right to feel these emotions, by helping them choose whether to keep them or to release them, by confronting false beliefs that justify their continuation of these emotions, and by choosing to release them. When naturalistic methods fail to release the individual from these emotions, they can be released by giving their feelings to God through prayer.

5.   Belief-based emotions can be logically challenged at times, but usually are resistant to change because they are rooted in earlier events that need to be identified.

6.   The original root-cause events can usually be identified by asking the client to focus on their strongest feeling and then try to remember the first time they felt this emotion. The client should be instructed to remain focused on the strong emotion until he remembers previous occasions when he felt a similar feeling.

7.   Once the root-cause event is found and the client remains focused on the strong negative emotions in that memory, the root-cause beliefs can be identified by asking the client how the event made him feel and by asking him why he felt this way.

8. Once the root-cause beliefs are identified in the original events they can be challenged through standard cognitive therapy techniques. However, historically-embedded, experiential beliefs are resistant to change and respond best to prayer-based techniques. Once they are effectively challenged the client will be able to talk about the original event without eliciting the strong negative emotion. If other negative emotions are still present during recall of the event, this process should be repeated with each of the other negative emotions connected to the same event.

9. Individuals who have suppressed or repressed their root-cause events will be unable to recall the earlier events until they are willing to remember them and experience the painful emotions connected to them. These painful memories often have layers of beliefs that must be systematically challenged before the person will be willing to remember the original event and challenge the wrong beliefs connected to it.

10. If an individual is unwilling to remember events from the past and to experience the painful feelings associated with them, he will not make further therapeutic progress until he makes a conscious choice to remember them. The process of making these choices is a dynamic that occurs repeatedly throughout each counseling session when probing for root events and root beliefs underlying the client's negative emotions.

11. The change process can be conducted either naturalistically, by focusing upon whatever emotion the client is currently experiencing, or systematically, by encouraging the client to systematically explore painful experiences in his/her life that are believed to have impacted him/her in a negative way.

12. Once painful experiences have been explored and the underlying beliefs have been thoroughly challenged or replaced with truth, the individual will no longer experience strong emotions when discussing that experience, and it will usually have a chain reaction by neutralizing similar experiences connected to that memory.

Basic Principles of Emotional Healing Prayer

1. Most emotions are the result of the beliefs and interpretations that we make of events around us. When God's truth fills our minds so that we interpret life events from His perspective we experience the "peace of God that surpasses comprehension."

2. Strong emotional reactions result when present circumstances resemble experiences we had in the past and trigger the root beliefs and negative emotions we had in those past experiences.

3. The emotions of grief, sadness, disappointment, guilt and legitimate anger are generally based upon truth, but the Lord is able and willing to replace these with His peace when we give them to Him and ask Him to carry them for us.

4. The emotions of aloneness, false shame, defilement, fear, hurt, helplessness, and hopelessness are based upon false beliefs and misinterpretations, and the underlying root lies must be replaced with truth by the Comforter in order for us to find freedom from these negative emotions.

5. There are two basic types of beliefs: surface beliefs and root beliefs. Surface beliefs can be modified through simple insights and logic, but only God is able to change root beliefs through His Holy Spirit.

6. Root beliefs are learned experientially and are the beliefs that directly control our emotional reactions, which often contradict our surface, intellectual beliefs about God and about ourselves.

7. In order to gain freedom from negative emotions based on root beliefs, we must be willing to face our emotions honestly and go through four basic steps: identify our emotions, identify the historical source of our emotions, identify the root beliefs connected to the memories, and pray for the Lord to replace the lies with His truth.

8. True mind renewal results when the Lord replaces our root beliefs with the truth, and leads to permanent changes in our emotional reactions when we revisit the original memories where the lies originated.

9. Many lies may be attached to a single memory, and each lie must be replaced with truth before true freedom and complete peace will be found in a memory.

10. God deliberately allows difficulties in our lives to expose our underlying lies, so that we can receive His deep inner truths and experience true mind renewal, genuine peace, and inner transformation.

11. Christians have a new divine nature and a desire to serve God, but need to have their minds renewed both on the surface and in their root beliefs to prevent them from being controlled by strong negative emotions. This mind-renewing process is a primary means by which God sanctifies His people and frees them to manifest the fruits of the Spirit.

BELIEF-BASED FEELINGS

"If any of you lacks wisdom, let him ask of God, who gives to all
generously and without reproach, and it will be given to him." James 1:5

Emotion	False Beliefs
Aloneness	"I'm all alone, no one cares about me, I'm abandoned, not even God cares about me, I will always be alone, no one understands me, God has forsaken me, there is no one to protect me, they will never come back for me."
False Shame	"I feel stupid, it was my fault, I should have done something to stop it, I participated in it, I enjoyed it, I deserved it, it happened because of my appearance, I should have resisted, I should have told someone, I am bad, dirty, and shameful."
Defilement	"I'm dirty and defiled because of what happened to me, everyone can tell that I am dirty, I'll never be clean again, no one will ever be able to love me after what I've done, my body is dirty, I will never be happy, even God could not want me or listen to me after what I've done."
Fear	"I'm going to die, I'm trapped, he is going to come back and hurt me again, something terrible is going to happen to me, I'm going to be hurt, if I tell anyone they will come back and hurt me again, it will destroy my family if I tell anyone, doom and despair are coming to me."
Hurt	"I am unimportant, I am not wanted, loved, or valued, my feelings are not important, I am worthless, no one cares for me, I cannot measure up no matter how hard I try, I am unacceptable, I cannot please others because _____, I was a burden, I am in the way, I am not liked, I am not appreciated, I am not affirmed or validated."
Helplessness	"I'm weak, I'm overwhelmed, I'm helpless against him, I cannot do anything to resist him, I'm too small to do anything about it, I'm going to die, everything is out of control, even God cannot help me, there is no way out."
Hopelessness	"There is no hope for me, it's never going to get better, there is no way out, not even God can help me, nothing good can ever come from this, I have no reason to live."
Confusion	"I don't know how I feel, it's all so confusing, I didn't know what to think, I was shocked and stunned, it doesn't make any sense, I don't know what is happening."

Note: This form is adapted from "Beyond Tolerable Recovery," by Ed Smith, 1999, p. 406.

FACT-BASED FEELINGS

"Casting all your cares upon Him, because He cares for you." 1 Peter 5:7

These five feelings are based upon facts or events that have occurred in an individual's life which cause pain, even if you have no distorted beliefs.

Emotion	*Scriptures and Principles*
Grief and Loss	"He was despised and forsaken of men, a man of sorrows and acquainted with grief....Surely our griefs He Himself bore, and our sorrows He carried" (Isaiah 53:3-4) "He was deeply moved in spirit and was troubled...Jesus wept." (John 11:33, 35)
Justified Anger	"And after looking around at them with anger, grieved at their hardness of heart, He said to the man, 'Stretch out your hand.' (Mark 3:5) "His anger is but for a moment...but a shout of joy comes in the morning." (Psalms 30:5) "Be angry, and yet do not sin; do not let the sun go down on your anger, and do not give the devil an opportunity." (Ephesians 4:26-27)
Sadness	"O Jerusalem, Jerusalem, the city that kills the prophets and stones those sent to her! How often I wanted to gather your children together, just as a hen gathers her brood under her wings, and you would not have it! Behold, your house is left to you desolate; and I say to you, you shall not see Me until the time comes when you say, 'Blessed is He who comes in the name of the Lord!'" (Luke 13:34-35) "When He approached, He saw the city and wept over it." (Luke 19:41)
Disappointment	"He reproached them for their unbelief and hardness of heart, because they had not believed those who had seen Him after He had risen." (Mark 16:14) "Now it came about when I heard these words, I sat down and wept and mourned for days; and I was fasting and praying before the God of heaven" (Nehemiah in Nehemiah 1:4)
Genuine Guilt	"When I kept silent about my sin, my body wasted away Through my groaning all day long. For day and night Thy hand was heavy upon me; My vitality was drained away as with the fever-heat of summer. I acknowledged my sin to Thee, And my iniquity I did not hide; I said, 'I will confess my transgressions to the Lord'; And Thou didst forgive the guilt of my sin." (David in Psalms 32:3-5)

Made in the USA
Lexington, KY
17 February 2013